READING RECOVERY

A GUIDEBOOK FOR TEACHERS IN TRAINING

MARIE M. CLAY

READING RECOVERY

A GUIDEBOOK FOR TEACHERS IN TRAINING

HEINEMANN

Published by Heinemann Education, a division of Reed Publishing (NZ) Ltd,
39 Rawene Road, Birkenhead, Auckland. Associated companies, branches and
representatives throughout the world.

In the United States: Heinemann, a division of Reed Publishing (USA) Inc.,
361 Hanover Street, Portsmouth, NH 03801-3912

ISBN 0 86863 289 9 (NZ)

© 1993, Marie M. Clay
First published 1993

Library of Congress Cataloging-in-Publication Data

Clay, Marie M.
   Reading recovery: a guidebook for teachers in training/Marie M.
Clay.
        p.   cm.
   Includes bibliographical references and index.
   ISBN 0-435-08764-9
   1. Reading—Remedial teaching.   2. Reading. teachers—Training of.
I. Title.
LB1050.5.C56   1993   93-24028
372.4' 3—dc20   CIP

Printed in Hong Kong

The pronouns she and he have often been used in this text to refer to the teacher
and the child respectively. Despite a possible charge of sexist bias it makes for
clearer, easier reading if such references are consistent.

The author and publishers permit the following observation record sheets to be
copied by teachers for use with children. The commercial use of any of these
observation record sheets is strictly prohibited.

* Weekly Record of Writing Vocabulary
* Lesson Record
* Recommendations for Discontinuing Children
* Observation Summary for Multiple Testings

CONTENTS

Three notes of caution

Most children (80 to 90 percent) do *not* require these detailed, meticulous and special Reading Recovery procedures or any modification of them. They will learn to read in classroom programmes of many different kinds. For a few children individual and consistent tutoring with these special procedures introduced after one year of instruction may well prevent the development of a pattern of reading failure.

It should be stressed that a Reading Recovery programme can be used with children from any kind of classroom programme, and in a brief period of help, supplementary to the ongoing activities of the classroom, it brings the hardest-to-teach children to a level where they can be full participants in that classroom programme. Because it is an individual intervention with only the hardest-to-teach children, Reading Recovery cannot specify how a classroom programme for children of wide-ranging abilities should be mounted. One would not design a classroom programme by studying the needs of the hardest-to-teach children.

Reading Recovery teachers need special training to make superbly sensitive decisions about how to interact with the responses of the hard-to-teach child. This book provides the conceptualisation of how and why the programme is the way it is, and it puts the main procedures into a text to be read. But how the teacher makes these procedures work for the individual learner with unusual patterns of responding or with limited expertise in necessary aspects of the task is something that defies recording in a linear script of words.

1 THE PREVENTION OF READING AND WRITING DIFFICULTIES

This book is a companion volume to *An Observation Survey of Early Literacy Achievement* (Clay, 1993). The Observation Survey introduces teachers to ways of observing children's progress in the early years of learning about literacy, and leads to the selection of children for whom supplementary teaching is essential. This volume is a guidebook for training Reading Recovery teachers to deliver such a supplementary programme. It addresses the hope and scope of an early intervention programme.

THREE STEPS TO PREVENTION

The first essential step towards reading and writing success is to have good preschool experiences available to all children. This would ensure that almost all children entered school easily able to converse with others about the world and how they understand it. Those who grow up in a literate environment will have prior knowledge about books and print to bring to school. Sometimes this prior knowledge will be about literacy in a language that is not English. Those who come to school from cultures where the emphasis is more on the oral tradition will have some backlog of literacy learning to catch up on, because printed language would not have had such an important place in their homes. The children who come to school speaking their home language fluently have a preparation for literacy learning that is to be valued even though some of them may now have to add to their language skills by learning the language of the school and their teacher. Experience tells us that children can add a second language at this time with relative ease; it just takes time, and hopefully they will be viewed as competent children who speak and problem-solve well in their first culture and who are tackling the learning of a second language earlier than most education systems require!

The second essential in the prevention of literacy problems is a good curriculum for literacy learning in the early years of school. Most children will learn to read in the first years of school (in Infant or Junior or First Grade programmes) if individual needs and personal learning schedules are taken into account.

Against the background of good preschool education and a sound classroom programme for five- to eight-year-olds it is possible to take a third important step towards reducing the numbers of children with difficulties in reading, writing and spelling by introducing an early intervention for children who are being left behind by fast-learning classmates. Such an early intervention seems to have the advantage of providing a window on an individual child's learning. Individually designed and individually delivered lessons can bring the child's progress back into the average band of achievement in a very short time. This third important step involves three things:

1 a check on the age group at the end of the first year of school
2 a second-chance programme for those who need it
3 specialist services for those very few whose problems persist after the intervention.

(See Clay, 1993 for further discussion of these issues.)

ON ENTRY TO SCHOOL

At the beginning of schooling when children enter formal instruction the foundations of all their future interactions with education are being laid. Children need to emerge from these years with a control of the language of instruction (and another language if they are fortunate enough to already speak one), well on the way to becoming the kind of reader whose reading improves because he reads, and on the way to becoming a writer. These language arts are the tools needed by the child for further educational progress, particularly in an information age.

What happens to the five-year-olds who come into schools? How are they grouped? When are they moved to another group? Or to a new class? What exactly happens about shifting groups of children from one class to another? These questions are related to the quality of instruction given to the school entrants. Each school knows what it does, but there is no description of what everyone else does and no evaluation of one practice against another. It would be interesting to compare schools, noting differences in organisation and differences in the criteria used for moving children. We would find different solutions in schools of different sizes. For example, in an education system with an admissions policy of continuous entry* the growth rate of a district would make a difference. If one school has new entrants coming at the rate of a whole new class a month it is going to have different kinds of problems and different solutions for class organisation from a school where one class fills up in the first six months or in the first year.

Countries decide on some arbitrary basis, for historical reasons, or custom, or convention, the age at which children start school. Once the large group of children is in a classroom then their lives will be different from what they would have been had they not come into formal education at that time. Simply bringing them into formal education, into a reception class, into developmental programmes, changes the life opportunities for those children. Whatever the child has been able to learn before he comes to school, whatever his behaviours are, whatever his response to his environment has been, his prior learning now goes through some transitions. The teacher in the reception class is trying to bring the children from those varied behaviours that they learned in their preschool years towards some behaviours shared with other children. The teacher is trying to encourage a transition from the behaviour that the child brings to school to some behaviour he can use in school on academic tasks. He may have limited language patterns and these have to be brought to something that can be worked on along with other children in a programme. He may be withdrawn, and his social behaviour may have to be brought to the point where he can work with a group.

Because we invite children into formal education we must give up the idea that 'they ripen and mature so that after a while they begin to read'. This is not true. Teachers and schools are engineering certain transitions. I think this concept is very important. It gets us away from the idea of the reception class teacher as one who is just minding the children until they mature, at which point

---

* School entry at any time in the year, as in New Zealand where entry is usually on the child's fifth birthday.

they can be moved on to a teacher who is really going to do some work with them. That is far from the true situation. If we look at the changes made by children in the reception class these transitions seem even more important than those made later in primary school. If teachers monitored these transitions sensitively and individualised their teaching for the slow-to-learn pupils as a result of those observations, they would be improving the quality of their teaching.

The entry class is most important. Where do reception class teachers learn their trade? How much help do they have when they first begin to teach children who are entering school? The more formal the school programme, engineered by the teacher to meet the education system's requirements, the more bewildered the new entrant child can become. If the teacher and the system take into account that the child's prior learning has not taught him:

- how to work with a large group of children
- how to obey institutional rules
- how to meet the minute-by-minute expectations of the teacher
- how to compete for her attention with other children

— in a word, how to interact with this new complex environment so as to profitably learn from it — then the teacher's way of organising and managing her room is likely to differ from the procedures which can succeed in higher classes, once children have learned how to act in school. One of my pleas would be that the teacher asked to take a new entrant class be someone with experience of young learners, and that an initial and continuing training period be provided for them as they adapt to the new task. For children this first year at school is a very important time.

In 1964 I watched children's progress through the first year of school by taking records at weekly intervals of what they were doing and what they were saying. To give two examples of the long-term outcomes of their progress, one of the boys who went along fairly slowly for the first six months ended up with marks over 90 per cent for six subjects in School Certificate (a national examination taken in the third year of secondary school). Another boy at the same school got into a terrible tangle in the first year, had severe reading problems, went to a reading clinic for several years and finally passed School Certificate. That was a success story for a child whose whole schooling had been a trouble to him because of the inappropriate learning that he did in the first year at school. At the end of this study I was saying that we ought to reduce our new entrant classes; we ought not to let them rise above 25 children. Now I would set that goal lower, at a maximum roll of 20 for the first year at school. The purpose of this is to meet each child where he is, arrange instruction so that he can proceed from his strengths and ensure that all children move into schooling without confusions, and with a sense of success.

In New Zealand we have children entering school throughout the year, on their fifth birthdays. We recognise that all children will need to be read to, and will want to participate in booksharing and storytelling and dramatised stories, as well as in attempts to write down messages and stories. These children will begin to read the print in their writing and in familiar story books at different rates, some almost on entry to school, others within a month or two months of entry, others not for half a school year and some children not until the end of the first year.

There is considerable variation in the rate at which New Zealand children move into simple little reading books. In my opinion, the explanation for these delays is not that the child is taking a year to mature but that he is taking a year to learn many things along several dimensions that contribute to reading and writing, and which lay the foundation of later success. Some children have learned many of these 'things' when they enter school, some take about six months to learn them, some take at least a year. We can pick up some children at six years of age who have not acquired effective control of these early reading and writing behaviours.

Here I want to add a critical note. Educators have individualised the rate at which they introduce children to programmes, but I do not believe we have paid sufficient attention to individualising the tasks and instruction that we provide during that period. It is not only that these children are moving at different rates; some of them need more help with some aspects of the task than others. We need to think more about children taking different paths to similar outcomes.

OBSERVING PROGRESS

To be able to detect how different the path has to be for some children we will have to observe a little more closely than we have in the past what the five- to six-year-old is doing and what he is capable of. Some of my work has been directed towards providing class teachers with some structured situations in which they can improve their observation of children's actual behaviour to record with greater accuracy what they can do, and by implication, what they cannot do (Clay, 1993).

If there is no magical moment at which a child is 'ready' what can we look for in the first year that indicates progress or lack of it? I look for movement or change in the child's behaviour. My criterion for progress during the first year of school would be that he moves from those responses he can give when he comes to school toward some other goals that I see as appropriate for him. I am looking for *movement in appropriate directions* and only careful monitoring will assure me that the child is not practising inappropriate behaviours. For if I do not watch what he is doing, and if I do not capture what is happening in records of some kind, Johnny, who never gets under my feet and who never comes really into a situation where I can truly see what he is doing, may, in fact, for six months or even a year, practise behaviours that will handicap him in reading.

One of the critical areas is directional behaviour. The boy who had some difficulty in getting School Certificate was a boy who was quite confused about direction (or serial order rules of the English language). At the end of the first year he would happily go from right to left as often as he would go from left to right. Visual learning in reading is nonsense if you do not happen to be looking at the print in the appropriate direction. But that is where he got to by the end of the first year at school — a rather consistent right to left visual survey of print. Organising for preventing reading failure depends a great deal on providing opportunities for observing what children are doing.

I would like to expand on this idea of observing. My emphasis on this came from my work as a researcher rather than from my work as a teacher. I decided that because the explanations in books did not seem to account for my successes with remedial work I would assume that I knew nothing about what reading is and what we should do in reading; I would adopt a neutral stance and observe exactly what children did. In taking this position I stepped out of a teaching role entirely and became much more like a scientist setting up a situation and recording precisely what happens. When I write of observing children closely this is what I mean. There must be times when the teacher stops teaching and becomes an observer, a time when she must drop all her presuppositions about what this child is like, and when she listens very carefully and records very precisely what the child can in fact do.

To prevent reading failure teachers must have time to observe what children are able to do. This means time out from teaching, time set aside for observing. The younger the child and the poorer the reader, the more time the teacher requires for observing and for thinking about what she observes. One must organise for such observation times. In this situation it is difficult not to prompt, not to help and not to teach. These activities do not have any place in the observation situation which is a completely different thing.

Observation involves more than hearing children read every day. It involves being a teacher who interacts with the child who is reading, attending not only to the story and its meanings, but also to how the child is working on print to get those understandings. The teacher must be reflective and responsive to the negotiations of the child.

A CHECK AFTER ONE YEAR AT SCHOOL

Knowing the pressures on teachers one has to be realistic about this. What would be the most economical time from the teacher's point of view to carry out thorough observation checks to catch up the children who are either confused or not making progress? I hope the class teacher would observe her children as often as possible, from week to week perhaps. But drastic changes occur in children's lives. Children change school or change classes, they lose parents who leave the home, they have intermittent absences for legitimate health reasons. It is not sufficient to leave the decision to observe or not, to the class teacher. Towards the end of the first year at school somebody should be responsible for checking on reading and writing behaviour.

Why do I recommend this at the end of the child's first year in New Zealand? It allows the checking process to go on all year, for it would be difficult to carry out this type of check on all children at the one time, say, at the end of a year. The child is given sufficient time to adjust to the school situation. The child who is slow to begin can be given a variety of opportunities to make progress. The teacher who finds that a certain focus within the programme does not suit the child can emphasise a different aspect. The sixth birthday check maximises the opportunities, minimises the pressure on the child, and does not leave the child for more than one year to practise bad habits that might handicap him and be very hard to unlearn. If you leave it until some of the children are 6:6 you have shortened the time for remedial help before the question of promotion to a higher class comes up. The longer we leave them without supplementary help, the shorter time we have, and the more they have practised inappropriate responding.

A check on progress after about a year at school (and sooner for the older school entrant) does call for organis-

ing. The teacher who supervises the early years of school might, in the first instance, do the evaluations herself, but she could then introduce her staff to the work of carrying this out. (The timing of such a survey will vary with the age of entry to school and other factors like promotion and assessment policies.) We must organise to observe the ways in which change in literacy learning is occurring after one year into school for five- and six-year-old beginners, and six months to one year into school for seven-year-old beginners. When we have applied the Observation Survey (Clay, 1993) and have found some children who are confused or not engaging well with literacy activities, we will need some very skilful teachers to teach children who have been defined by the observation procedures as children in need of special help. Inexperienced teachers will not work as well with the children selected who have ways of responding which are hard to understand. The children with special needs will be hard to teach. The teacher needs experience with children who make normal progress so that she understands that there are different paths to similar outcomes, and she must have the flexibility to do different things with different children. Within a school this calls for organising so that you can have staff with special expertise available for the children sorted out by the early intervention check on progress.

Teachers who work in such an early intervention programme should be given recognition for the kind of job they are able to do. The task is not quite as exciting as teaching children of varied talents in a classroom. It is a job that carries more strain, and one's pupils will, inevitably, have lower achievement than those of other teachers at the end of the year. The school has to recognise that this person is very important and needs appropriate rewards for tackling this task. The response of these children may not be rapid, even when they are given a highly skilled and experienced teacher who uses special techniques. Not all of them will make a spurt in that second year and 'catch up'. The children who do this will be the ones who have not really taken much notice of the programme in the first year and who now begin to take notice and to learn. Most children who have made little progress by six years are children who have difficulty in learning spontaneously what most children learn but who can become literate with extra teaching directed to their idiosyncratic needs.

What can one look for in early reading in order to prevent failure? Let me make an analogy with mathematics and the changes we have seen there in the last few years. Almost nobody considering the young child moving into learning maths is going to think in terms of how many arithmetical items he knows. Almost everybody will be thinking: 'What mathematical operations can he carry out?' Although we may not yet have definitive descriptions of the strategies or operations used or to be acquired in early literacy this is the kind of shift in our thinking we have to make.

In order to prevent early struggles with literacy learning *we should be trying to understand the strategies the child is using.* We have to observe him reading book material as well as checking on his word recognition. We can hear a child correcting himself as he reads. As he is reading along, he stops, he goes back. Nobody suggested that he should do this. This is a strategy that tells us he is monitoring his own reading. If he is listening to what he is saying he has recognised that something does not fit, goes back, and takes responsibility for working on it.

The high-progress readers move into reading, they get certain help and then by the time they have been at school about a year, they are monitoring their own reading in helpful ways. On texts which interest and challenge them they can teach themselves new things for working on that new material.

The child who is not able to do this monitoring of his own reading is the one who needs the teacher most. Observation records made by teachers show that they allow good readers to read much more than they do slow readers. There are reasons why this occurs. The slow child takes longer to read, and he is reading much more limited text. The high-progress reader is reading involved text and reads many pages to get through an important part of the story. If there is anything in this about organising, it suggests that if we simply organise to give the slow children twice as much time as the good readers we might in fact be doing quite a lot for the prevention of reading failure.

So it is important to look for strategies, to look for progress in the child's reading strategies, and particularly to see that children are getting to the point where they can tutor themselves. Situations must be set up where they can carry on without much attention from the teacher. This leaves her more time to work with readers making slower progress.

ADVANTAGES OF INDIVIDUAL INSTRUCTION

A major problem in thinking about what school organisation will improve the quality of instruction is the individ-ual learner versus the group instruction dilemma. Formal education procedures are, of necessity, group procedures, but the best progress for a particular child will result from individual instruction. A compromise between the large class procedure and the individual one is to group children. This is our dilemma. How do we meet individual learning needs even under group instruction procedures? One cannot justify teaching all children on the assumption that all need the same kind of teaching. Teachers do recognise the great differences between children, and within children, and in their background experiences and personality traits.

The need for organising reading instruction in order to provide in an adequate way for individual differences is recognised but much still remains to be done in practical application. This implies different programmes for different children, not just an expectation that children will progress through the same programme at a different rate.

There was a strong emphasis on individual tuition in the education system in Sweden in the early 1970s. One of the main regulations of the Swedish Education Act of 1962 and 1969 was that the personal resources of the individual child must not only be respected but must be the starting point for the planning of education and teaching. According to objectives stated in the school law the school must stimulate the child's personal growth towards his development as a free, self-active, self-confident, harmonious human being. The school *must* give individual education.

Some steps taken in Sweden to further a diagnostic approach and the individualisation of the teaching of reading were:

- Class size was reduced to a maximum of 25 in the first three years — but the average size for the country as a whole for the first three years lay between 17 and 18 children per class.
- Better opportunities than before were provided for individual tutoring, small group teaching, teaching in clinics and by offering special classes of various kinds.
- In the first three grades, there was written into the teaching load of each teacher a weekly two-hour block of time for tutoring individual children from her class who, in her judgement, needed such help. Obviously there had to be organisation for this when it was part of the teacher's weekly work.
- Another procedure aimed at the individualisation of teaching was to have one-half of the reception class or first-year class meet with the teacher for the first two hours of the day, with the second half arriving two

hours later and staying on two hours later. This is an interesting way to reduce numbers and allow more individual instruction for children having particular difficulties.

To prevent literacy problems, observation of children's early interactions with print, and individual teaching for some children are recommended.

IN SUMMARY

To help those children who are clearly getting left behind by the end of their first year at school, we do have to organise:

- For using strengths of teaching staffs at appropriate points.
- For new teaching staff to have opportunities to gain these strengths by observing people who are expert in working with them.

- For opportunities to see precisely how the child is working on texts and how to support his progress.
- For identifying children who need supplementary help to build a sound foundation for literacy learning.
- To give more individual attention and teacher time to those children who are making slow progress in reading and/or writing.

There will always be a challenge to meet individual differences when children enter school because at that time children are very different in so many ways. Teachers must be observant of individuals' responses and of individual progress. They must be aware of the alternate learning sequences which can lead to progress, and they must know when progress is not occurring. Organising effectively for meeting individual needs in the first year of school is important, *especially* for children who are slow to move into the classroom programme which the school has selected for beginning reading. By the second year a small number of children who need special supplementary help can be identified.

2 REDUCING READING AND WRITING DIFFICULTIES WITH A SECOND CHANCE TO LEARN

Whatever their origins, reading and writing difficulties have a large learned component. They limit achievement in school learning. They get worse if untreated and many pupils get further behind their classmates over time even when they receive available treatments. Surprisingly, although what is difficult about reading differs markedly from child to child the programmes they have been placed in have often been prescriptive and general.

If the young school entrant has not been able to learn in the classroom programme after one year at school, what happens if the education system organises to provide him with individual instruction each day in a programme which starts with what he can do and takes him along his own particular route into reading and writing? At the organisational level that is what the Reading Recovery programme does. Research (see Chapter 6) has shown that a large percentage of children who were the poorest readers in their schools after one year at school responded quickly to such an approach. Resources saved by the rapid progress of these children to average levels of performance can be directed to the very small percentage who need help for a longer term.

Reading Recovery is based on two assumptions. The first is that a programme for a child having difficulty learning to read should be based on a detailed observation of that child as a reader and writer, with particular attention to what that child can do. The programme will work out of these strengths and not waste time teaching anything already known. The second assumption is that we need to know

- how children who become readers learn to read
- how children who become writers learn to write.

Understanding this we are then in a better position to help children who are having difficulty. The progressions will vary slightly from one education system to another depending on the programmes and the ways in which they are delivered.

A STARTING POINT

My research observations of successful children learning to read have, over the years, led to my view of reading acquisition expressed in *Becoming Literate: The Construction of Inner Control* (Clay, 1991a). This is a general theory of learning to read which makes several assumptions.

- It assumes that a theory of reading continuous texts cannot arise from a theory of word reading because it involves the integration of many behaviours not studied in a theory of reading words. (It must, of course, explain the role of word reading and letter recognition within the theory of reading continuous text.)
- It assumes that the child begins to read by attending to many different aspects of printed texts (letters, words, pictures, language, messages, stories) with limited knowledge and primitive response patterns which change in two ways: 1) learning about each of these areas expands; 2) ways of working on the interrelationships of these areas develop.
- It assumes that tasks which require the learner's close attention at first gradually require less and less attention (unless some local problem arises and needs to be solved). This means that what reading involves, what the reader is attending to, and how his mind is working on the task probably changes over the first years of literacy learning to enable the beginning reader, reading slowly and aloud, to become the fluent, fast silent reader who is about nine years of age. There is change

over time, not only in what is known, but also in how reading is carried out.

The observation procedures outlined in the Observation Survey (Clay, 1993) provide a basis for describing what a particular child has learned about reading and writing, and to some extent, what changes are occurring in the way the reader works on texts.

Longitudinal observation of children in the first years of school reveals children who are low in achievement compared with their average classmates. This may occur for many different reasons. Experience with the Reading Recovery programme shows that many of these children can respond to a supplementary programme in such a way that they can catch up to their average classmates. So the general theory about learning to read described above can be played out in a particular way to address this problem. From the general theory two distinct sets of implications for teaching can follow: one for classroom practice with children making successful progress in the school's programme, and another for the children who are the lowest achievers in the age group, not excluding any child in an ordinary classroom for any reason.

What is required for a second-chance programme for these lowest achievers?

INDIVIDUAL INSTRUCTION

The gains recorded for the Reading Recovery programme have been made with individual instruction. It sounds like an expensive approach but has proved to be economical for two reasons. Firstly, many children move through the programme very quickly, on average in 12 to 15 weeks, and their places are then taken by other children. Secondly, after leaving the programme almost all the children have been able to move forward with average children in their classes over the next three years and very few have needed further help. There is therefore a saving in special education costs. The economy lies in mounting a high-quality programme.

Why is a switch to individual instruction so powerful in its effects? It allows for a revolutionary change in teaching, devising lessons which work out from the things the child can already do, and not from the teacher's preselected programme sequence. When two or three children are taught in a group the teacher cannot make this change; she has to choose a compromise path, a next move for 'the group'. To get results with the lowest achievers the teacher must work with the particular (and very limited) response repertoire of a particular child

using what he knows as the context within which to introduce him to novel things.

Individual instruction also allows the child who does not know when his attempts are good and when they are poor to be reinforced by the teacher immediately he makes an appropriate response. The teacher's close supervision will also allow her to detect an interfering or handicapping type of response when it creeps in, and to swiftly arrange for a better response to occur. She may structure the task (for example, provide a masking card or a pointer) or she may note the need to teach some new basis for making choices between words. Throughout the 30-minute lesson the teacher's attention is tuned to the responding history of this one child. One teacher per pupil is the only practical way of working with children who have extreme difficulty in learning to read.

The result of individual programming is that programmes differ from child to child.

ACCELERATION

The child requiring help with early reading and writing has been making very slow progress and has been dropping further and further behind his classmates. In order to become an average-progress child he would have to make fast progress, faster than his classmates, to catch up to them. Acceleration refers to this rate of progress.

To say that the slow-progress child who cannot be pushed or placed under stress should now learn at an accelerated rate seems to be a puzzling contradiction. However, I have already discussed two important factors which help this to occur. He will get one-to-one teaching and the programme will start with his strengths and proceed according to what *he* is able to discover about reading and writing. He will get help but his teacher will follow his lead.

In addition, whenever possible the child will read and write text. He will not be diverted from printed texts to pictorial material or puzzles but will be taught what he needs to learn in the context of continuous text. (There might be good reasons for a rare exception to this.) The new letter or a high-frequency word or a spelling pattern is used in the same lesson in text reading and text writing, and the learner interacts with the teacher about the relationships of detail to continuous text.

Acceleration depends upon how well the teacher selects the clearest, easiest, most memorable examples with which to establish a new response, skill, principle or procedure. For example, the child trying to recall how to use the 'ing' verb ending may be helped by the first example of an 'ing' word that he learned. The teacher needs to select examples which are very productive: that means they occur often or relate easily to many other things. Productive examples lead to further reading or writing control in a number of different ways.

With problem readers it is not enough for the teacher to have rapport, to generate interesting tasks and generally to be a good teacher. The teacher must be able to design a superbly sequenced programme determined by the child's performance, and to make highly skilled decisions moment by moment during the lesson.

The child must never engage in unnecessary activities because that wastes learning time. If the teacher judges that a child can make a small leap forward, she must watch the effects of this decision and take immediate supportive action if necessary. An expert teacher will help the child to leap appropriately; she will not walk the child through a preconceived sequence of learning step by step.

Acceleration is achieved as the child takes over the learning process and works independently, discovering new things for himself inside and outside the lessons. He comes to push the boundaries of his own knowledge, and not only during his lessons. The teacher must watch for and use this personal searching on the part of the child.

Achieving acceleration is not easy but it must be constantly borne in mind. During Reading Recovery training a teacher is challenged if she seems to be wasting the learner's time, especially when her peers notice that she is teaching something the child has already shown that he can do!

Two kinds of learning must be kept in balance: on the one hand there is performing with success on familiar material which strengthens the decision-making processes of the reader as he works across text, and on the other there is independent problem-solving on new and interesting texts with supportive teaching. Texts need to be chosen with these two kinds of learning in mind. Both will contribute to acceleration.

The teacher will foster and support acceleration as she moves the child quickly through his programme, making superb decisions and wasting no unnecessary time, but the teacher cannot produce or induce it. *The teacher cannot decide that the time has come and she will now accelerate the rate of progress*. It is the learner who accelerates because some things which no longer need his attention are done more easily, freeing him to attend to new things. When this happens at an ever-increasing rate acceleration of learning occurs.

DAILY INSTRUCTION, INTENSIVE PROGRAMME

Reading Recovery lessons are given daily. In that way even the child who cannot remember from day to day can be helped. The teacher acts as the memory of what his response was yesterday, and prompts him accordingly. (Twice-weekly lessons are a weak approach to meeting special learning needs. Twice a week with a group of children *makes it impossible* to design the programme to meet the needs of the individual learner.)

The power of the programme to effect change is diminished

- when the child is not attending regularly (and therefore Reading Recovery teachers contract with parents before the programme begins to have the child at school)
- when the teacher is not available to teach (because she is ill, allocated other duties, away on inservice courses).

When daily, intensive programming is not achieved the quality of the teaching and the outcomes of the programme are seriously affected.

The principles of an intensive programme allow the close supervision of the shifts in the child's responding. Short lessons held often are important for success. This allows the learning to be carried over from one day to the next.

GETTING DOWN TO DETAIL

In learning to read the child making normal progress picks up and organises for himself a wealth of detailed information about letters, print, words and reading with a spontaneity that leads teachers to believe that many things do not have to be taught. There is evidence that this attention to print in the environment, in books, and in early attempts to write begins early in the preschool years for some children. Others, however, may have given it little thought.

From time to time the child having difficulty in learning to read may have to pay attention to the detail of print. Letter learning must be done, *although book reading can begin when only a few letters are known*. There will be a gradual accumulation of letter knowledge as the child reads and writes. Some children will need particular attention to letter formation, not 'to get it right' from the point of view of good writing but because these few children cannot analyse the form into its parts, or cannot find a learned routine for producing it.

If a child knows most of the letters one cannot assume that he has access to this knowledge while reading continuous text. One of the problems often encountered is a child not seeing any relationship between letters he recognises in isolation and what he is looking at in continuous text in a reading book. He has yet to learn how to use one source of knowledge in another context.

And, if the children selected for this programme seem to be reading quite well, one cannot assume that letter learning will 'fall into place' as it seems to do with children making average progress.

When the teacher becomes involved in teaching for detail the principle of acceleration is seriously threatened. (So also is the child's ability to use his language knowledge and the meaning of the text, as part of his information base for decision-making.) The child cannot afford to spend much time practising detail, and he may become addicted to such practice and find it difficult later to take a wider approach to the reading act. *Tuition on detail* may aim to fill a small gap, or to clear a confusion; it *should be a detour from a programme whose main focus is reading books and writing stories.* The detour may be taken to pay attention to some particular aspect of print in the clear realisation that knowledge of the detail is of very limited value on its own. It must in the end be used in the service of reading or writing continuous text. Details must receive attention but always in a subsidiary status to message-getting.

TEACHING SEQUENCES

Every school and classroom has some teaching sequence by which reading is presented to children. For the child who has become a reading failure in that setting it will probably not be sufficient to change to a different teacher, different material and a different approach to instruction.

This remedy is often suggested, but I have not found it sufficient. Failing children differ more among themselves in response to curriculum than average children. They are a heterogeneous group whose strengths and weaknesses are different and whose learning tangles may need quite different programme details to untangle them. Programmes and teaching sequences of any standard kind are unlikely to meet the needs of severely retarded readers. While a commercial kit may be a slight improvement on nothing, the ideal programme will have activities individually selected to meet the needs of a particular child.

It therefore rests with the teacher to know the way in which reading skill develops, the teaching sequences that are possible and the short-cuts that are permissible. To be able to pick and choose among teaching techniques and learning activities, the teacher must be very familiar with her subject. *An experienced classroom teacher brings a great deal of knowledge to her Reading Recovery training because she has an inner awareness of the progressions in the classroom programme around which she can vary her particular lessons.* She has some sense of the endpoint and can bring the learners by different routes to similar outcomes.

Most school programmes will have established a series of books as the gradient of difficulty through which their children progress, and they refer to children's progress levels in terms of such books. Other programmes may leave children free to read story books, graded roughly for difficulty, and will assess progress by some other means, such as a standardised text or an informal prose inventory on a graded set of text material.

A Reading Recovery teacher wishing to bring her students to the levels of achievement of their average classmates will need to have some sequence of difficulty through which she attempts to move her students. Our programme uses many different books but an attempt is made to grade these simple story books against some benchmark series. A book may be selected because it can contribute to a particular child's learning problem of the moment but the teacher knows the level at which that book can be equated to the benchmark series. The instruction needs to be related to the progressions in the reading series used in the school or the classroom programme, but it need not take place on that series of books. Teachers can keep a child for weeks on one level, choosing books of parallel difficulty until the child is ready for the next step. On the other hand the teacher may help the child to jump forward two or three levels, support his initial uncertainty and be able to conclude that the acceleration was justified. In both these cases the child would not usually be reading the graded material of the classroom series but material known to be of equivalent difficulty (see Clay, 1993).

RECIPROCAL GAINS OF READING AND WRITING

The child who has failed to learn to read is often also struggling to write stories. Often remedial lessons exclude the teaching of writing as this is seen either as some extension that comes after reading or as a different subject. An alternative view sees both reading and writing in the early acquisition stage as contributing to learning about print. (They are separated by educators for timetables and curricula.) A case can be made for the theory that learning to write letters, words and sentences actually helps the child to make the visual discriminations of detail in print that he will use in his reading (Clay, 1982).

Children in Reading Recovery write stories every day. It is in the writing part of the daily lesson that children are required to pay attention to letter detail, letter order, sound sequences, letter sequences, and the links between messages in oral language and messages in printed language. It is particularly important that children learn to hear the sounds in words they want to write, and find appropriate ways to write these sounds down. The writing knowledge serves as a resource of information that can help the reader. However, this reciprocity does not occur spontaneously. The teacher must remember to direct the child to use what he knows in reading when he is writing and vice versa. The child comes to control a high-frequency vocabulary for writing and learns strategies for spelling more and more words in his language. Reading and writing are interwoven throughout the Reading Recovery programme and teaching proceeds on the assumption that both provide cues and responses which facilitate new responding in either area.

The simple 'stories' or sentences which Reading Recovery children write are viewed critically by some educators. They want these children to run before they can crawl. Daily writing shared with the teacher helps these children to understand more about the task, to learn to compose (simple though the composition may be), and to emerge from their programme with great resources for making the most of writing opportunities in the classroom.

Reading knowledge tends to draw ahead of writing knowledge after a while but at the beginning of school what the child can write is a good indicator of what the child knows in detail about written language.

3 | THE SHAPE OF THE READING RECOVERY CHILD'S PROGRAMME

Do you know how reading is taught in your school? Do you know what reading processes are being trained in those children who succeed? You ought to. It is important information for anyone to have if they are to try to make judgements about the reading problems of the other pupils in the same school. Any reading programme has its 'risk areas'. Any reading programme stresses some facets of the reading process and must as a consequence give less attention to other aspects. The teacher in Reading Recovery is trying to help her students to gain the same competencies as the successful children, and she needs to know how successful children behave.

Early intervention calls for sensitive observation of the children making slow progress, taking into account the competencies being acquired by the children making satisfactory progress in the classroom, and in the light of clear descriptions of the teaching, the day-to-day activities, and the sequential progressions of the programme.

For Reading Recovery we do not need an elaborate definition of reading difficulties. *One simply takes the pupil from where he is to somewhere else.*

Three assumptions are made in the outline that follows. The first is that a classroom programme will continue alongside the extra tuition. The second is that the extra tutoring will be individual. And the third is that the teacher will have been appropriately trained, meaning that she will not only understand the theory of the reading process upon which the programme is based but will be able to deliver instruction within the framework of that theory to the lowest achievers in the age group.

PREDICTIONS OF PROGRESS

Complete an Observation Survey (Clay, 1993) on a child and write up an Observation Summary Statement of the child's literacy competencies. This will provide guidance about where to begin planning his programme. To further direct the individual programme which the teacher will design it is necessary to make some predictions of progress.

Making 'predictions of progress' for a particular child will help a teacher keep a long-term perspective on her day-to-day decisions. Specify programme goals for each child. Look at what this particular child can do now and think about what he needs to learn to do. Consider the changes you would expect to see in the reading and writing behaviour of this child as he becomes a more competent reader and writer. Predict the paths of progress for each of the children entering your programme describing the changes in terms of the strategies you would expect them to acquire. Look at each Observation Survey Summary sheet, especially at the cues used and cues neglected and the problem and useful strategies sections.

The predictions should look like this:

- At the end of the teaching programme he will need to know how to . . . in order to . . .

listing as many strategies (or how to's) as are appropriate.

A concluding paragraph should be in this form:

- In the next few weeks he will need to know how to . . . and extra work will be needed on . . .

Record these predictions on a separate piece of paper and attach this to the Observation Summary Statement. Then a teacher can regularly evaluate a child's progress against these predictions in order to continue to make effective teaching decisions.

ROAMING AROUND THE KNOWN

For the first two weeks of the tutoring programme stay with what the child already knows. Do not introduce *any* new items of learning. The Observation Survey will have shown up some of the things that the child can do. During the first two weeks watch for and record other behaviours that you notice.

Go over what he knows in different ways until your ingenuity runs out, and until he is moving fluently around this personal corpus of responses, the letters, words and messages that he knows how to read or write.

There are several reasons why this period of roaming around the known makes a good starting point for the child's Reading Recovery programme.

- The observation techniques are only sampling procedures and this period gives the teacher a further opportunity to observe more of the child's ways of responding.
- The child and the teacher have an opportunity to get to know each other.
- The teacher is free to observe the child without the need to record all that occurs or think particularly of programme implications.
- The teacher works with reading texts and writing texts (and not with letters or words in isolation). This seems to give the child a feeling that he is 'really reading and writing'.
- The child may discover responses that he did not think he knew and in an unpressured situation he may observe new relationships.
- At the end of the period the child will feel comfortable with a small body of knowledge, confident enough to use this as a springboard for trying new things when the programme starts. This is a firm foundation on which the teacher can build.

However, the most important reason for roaming around the known is that it requires the teacher to stop teaching from her preconceived ideas. She has to work from the child's responses. This will be her focus throughout the programme.

Find a readable text

Find several appropriate texts that the child can read at about 90 percent accuracy or better. Do not guess. Measure this by taking a Running Record, even if it is only for a couple of lines of print. In your search for a simple text which the child can read, the following are suggestions for texts *which get easier as you go down the list.*

- an easy book
- a simple book about the child's own experiences
- a very simple story that you have read to this pupil
- a simple story that you write for this pupil keeping to his known vocabulary
- a simple text he has dictated.

Each of these is moving one step closer to the child's limited horizons. The better he is the further up the sequence you can start. The poorer he is the lower down that sequence you should start. You cannot rely on a published sequence of material for these earliest lessons. *The teacher must be the expert chooser and sequencer of the texts for a Reading Recovery pupil—this is critical.*

Think about the child's responses

Use the first two weeks of lessons to find out how the child responds in a teaching relationship. Make yourself specify just how he responds. Put it into words. What does he do well? What strategies does he try? How does he help himself? What more have you noticed about the letters, words and other features of print that he knows?

Encourage writing

Add to the information from the Observation Survey by finding out more about what he can write out of his head. Record what he can do. At all times keep records of what you discover that he can do.

Build fluency on the very little he knows

Hold his interest, bolster his confidence, make him your co-worker. Get the responding fluent and habituated but even at this stage encourage flexibility, using the same knowledge in different ways. Confidence, ease, flexibility and, with luck, discovery are the keynotes of this period which I have called 'roaming around the known'. Do not move too soon; be sure the foundation is firm and the child confident. Both the child and the teacher should be straining at the leash and wanting to go further, but resist the temptation. Most children need this two-week period before the teacher begins to introduce them to new learning.

New behaviours may appear

Now you will probably notice some things emerging that you did not think the child knew. New and useful behaviours appear as he begins to relate things one to another. He remembers a book with this or that in it. A letter reminds him of his uncle's name. He reads *car* for *are* or some such mismatch that makes you feel he is getting closer to effective decisions about uncertainty.

There are two reasons for this appearance of new behaviours. The child has many strategies which he uses to solve problems in his daily life. He is now beginning to apply these to reading. Why didn't he do this before? When one is having difficulty with a task one tries several approaches. As each fails one ceases to try them. The struggling reader has stopped using many strategies because he could not make them work. If you pitch the text at an easy level and you support him in using the things he can do you will find that he begins to try again some of these discarded strategies. You should show delight at this spontaneous relating of 'this to that'.

So you unleash those discarded approaches this child has ceased to use on the text. You probably could not achieve this if you used a standard or published pro-gramme. But you will have more luck if you are respond-ing to the child in an individual instruction situation. It only works well if the child's own capacities determine the programme.

Lessons 'in the known' may or may not look like a typical tutoring session. In order to stay with what the child already knows the teacher will share more of the tasks, repeat activities, create ingenious innovations and leave out some lesson components.

MOVING INTO INSTRUCTION

A typical tutoring session

In Reading Recovery a typical tutoring session would include each of these activities, usually in the following order, as the format of the daily lesson:

• rereading two or more familiar books	text
• rereading yesterday's new book and taking a running record	text
• letter identification (plastic letters on a magnetic board) *and/or* word-making and breaking	words and letters
• writing a story (including hearing and recording sounds in words)	text sounds
• cut-up story to be rearranged	text
• new book introduced	text
• new book attempted	text

There are several reasons for placing the new book at the end of the lesson, although some teachers have argued that the child is tired by this stage. Individual variations in lesson plans are always possible, providing there is a sound rationale based on a particular child's response to lessons.

The main reason for placing the new book at the end of the lesson is that each previous activity has encouraged the child to work on his own problems and to actively engage in problem-solving. By the end of the lesson he should have revised easy reading, letter knowledge, links between letters and sounds, his monitoring strategies in the cut-up story, and he should tackle his new book with his repertoire of responses in their most accessible form.

The second reason is that any new learning required for the new book can be introduced and practised during the other segments of the lesson.

The third reason for this placement of the new book is that there will be a minimum of interference between this timing and the rereading of the book the next day.

Introducing new material

At this stage there are some useful guidelines which help to keep the task easy.

• Make sure the child can hear a distinction or difference between two sounds or two words before you teach him to *see* the difference.
• Start with large units not the smallest ones
  — separate words out of phrases
  — separate letters out of words.
• Encourage the use of hand and eye together. The use of the eyes alone comes later in the learning sequence.
• Link something the child does easily with something he finds hard (for support) before asking for the difficult response on its own.
• Teach by demonstration. Use a questioning approach only for established responses.
• Aim to teach a few *items* (letters, words, sounds) and then try to establish further examples by *strategies of comparison*. Teaching all the items in a category is a teacher's hang-up. What the child needs to know is a few items and some strategies for picking up new ones later, as he reads.

Confusions

Now turn to the child's confusions. Without increasing the difficulty level and keeping to text reading, record and think about this particular child's confusions. Plan an attack on them. Talk to another couple of teachers about the easiest way to go from where he is to less confusion. That way you will find out what a blinkered approach each of us has to these difficulties and to teaching sequences. Probably you and your colleagues will not agree. Never mind. You have added their hypotheses to your own and can now approach the child's confusions tentatively, and with an open mind. With Reading Recovery cases do not rely on your own hunches. Be objective and critical of your own assumptions.

Some pointers about confusions are:

- Don't present them side by side. Get Item A well established and known for several weeks before you bring back Item B.
- Don't teach by the least noticeable difference principle. That is not the way we play the 'guess what I'm thinking about' games like 'Twenty Questions' or 'Animal, Vegetable or Mineral'.
- Is the child's difficulty in *seeing* a difference? If so, have him dictate, write, cut up and reassemble texts.
- Is the child's difficulty in *hearing* a difference? If so, articulate for him and with him very slowly, and teach him to use this strategy himself.
- Is the child's difficulty with order or sequence? If so, get him to dictate, read, cut up and reassemble and write a simple text.

You will probably have to move away from texts and into detail at this point. Resolve that this is a *temporary but necessary detour*, and plan to get back to text reading as soon as possible, preferably within the same lesson.

Developing a self-extending system

Plan to encourage a self-extending system and reinforce this.

- Give the child ways to detect error for himself.
- Encourage attempts to correct error.
- Give him clues to aid self-correction.
- Allow him to make checks or repetitions so he can confirm his first attempts.
- When he works out a word or text for himself, help him to know how he did it. Ask him 'How did you know?' (See page 38.)

Increasing text difficulty

Cautiously increase the text difficulty and repeat the sequence. Give massive practice on texts at this next level before you increase the difficulty level again.

Now look at what he cannot do

When the child is moving into higher-level texts offer him many things to stimulate various approaches to print. Pay particular attention to what you think would have the greatest payoff. This might be:

- an intensive vocabulary spree
- a training in predicting what structures come next
- a training in hearing sound sequences, first and last sounds and clusters of sounds

- a shift from sounding to syllabic attack
- letter identification.

Get those two colleagues together again and listen to their ideas on priorities and the way to achieve them. That exposes your assumptions to critical analysis. Keep the principles used in the games 'Twenty Questions' or 'Animal, Vegetable or Mineral', in mind.

Now go back to your pupil and ask him what he would like to learn next. Try to work this in with your priorities.

Some organisational points

Keep all those processes going *but* arrange for massive opportunity to read enchantingly interesting texts of just the right difficulty, over a longer period than anyone anticipated — and after the child and parents and class teacher want you to stop. Be conservative about recommending an end to supplementary help.

Developing effective strategies

Reading Recovery procedures have sometimes been questioned because they appear to require correct responding from children. This is not true.

There is a particular opportunity for revision and reworking in the one-to-one teaching situation. Child and teacher are talking about the reading or the writing as it occurs. There is opportunity for the child to initiate dialogue about his response as he works and for the teacher to help in many different ways. However, the programme sets the highest value on independent responding, and this must involve risks of being wrong. What the teacher will do is set some priorities as to which kinds of new learning she will attend to — just one or two things — and let the other behaviours that were incorrect go unattended at this time.

The goal of the teaching is to assist the child to produce effective strategies for working on text, not to accumulate items of knowledge. It is necessary to develop self-correction by allowing room for self-correction to be initiated by the child. A teacher who allowed only for correct responding would not be allowing the child to learn self-correcting behaviours!

Any theoretical position which includes self-monitoring and self-correcting as significant behaviour in reading or in writing implies the existence of near misses, uncorrected responses and sometimes corrected responses. The important thing about the self-corrections is that the child initiates them because he sees that something is wrong and calls up his own resources for working on a solution.

ROCHELLE'S PROGRESS BOOKS READ, BOOK LEVEL AND DIFFICULTY LEVEL				
Week of programme	Title		How difficult* was the book for the child?	Equivalent 'Ready to Read' Book Level**
1-4	(22 Titles)[1]		(No accuracy records)	
5	Cuckoo In The Nest	(PM)	Easy	3
5	Merry-Go-Round (plus 1 title)	(PM)	Easy	3
7	The Fire Engine (plus 1 title)	(R-to-R)	Easy	5
7	Planes (plus 1 title)	(PM)	Easy	5
8	The Escalator	(Star)	Easy	6
8	Going To School	(R-to-R)	Instructional	7
10	Playtime	(R-to-R)	Easy	8
10	Christmas Shopping (plus 1 title)	(R-to-R)	Easy	9
10	Saturday Morning (plus 2 titles)	(R-to-R)	Easy	10
11	The Christmas Tree (plus 1 title)	(PM)	Easy	11
11	Painting The Shed	(R-to-R)	Easy	11
12	A Country School (plus 1 title)	(R-to-R)	Easy	12
13	The Pet Show (plus 1 title)	(R-to-R)	Easy	13
14	At The Camp (plus 1 title)	(R-to-R	—	—
16	A Wet Morning (plus 1 title)	(PM)	Instructional	14
16	The Little Red Bus	(PM)	Instructional	13
16	The Pets Run Away (plus 4 titles)	(Playtime)	Instructional	14

* Easy: 95–100% accuracy achieved
Instructional: 90–94% accuracy achieved
Hard: below 90% accuracy.

** Equated to the graded series, 'Ready to Read'. This is a post hoc rating. The wide range of supplementary and story books used were not graded for equivalence to levels in the 'Ready to Read' series until 1980 (Watson, 1980).

1 This refers to other books read but not named here.

An example of reading book progress

Rochelle had almost a full programme of tutoring but may have been discontinued at too low a level. She made steady progress in the following year but three years later her progress was slower than average. She had 17 weeks in tutoring and only 41 lessons (obviously not a daily programme). She entered the programme at Red 1 level (New Zealand Ministry of Education 'Ready to Read' books, 1963) and at that time was just beginning to recognise words in text. Rochelle read 22 little books before she began her climb up through the reading levels. At each level she read several story books. Her teacher usually recorded her accuracy in the 'benchmark' books, the 'Ready to Read' books, and those are what are recorded in the table. The teacher's choice of books and her timing of the increase in difficulty level show excellent judge-

ment and good pacing of her pupil.

Rochelle's pattern of progress should not be taken as a model. Each child's selection of books, rate of progress, starting and finishing points will be different. All that Rochelle's record shows is how the shape of a Reading Recovery programme worked out for one child.

CHANGES THAT MAY OCCUR IN EACH SLOT OF THE DAILY LESSON

The table opposite provides some suggestions as to how the child's behaviour may change as the programme progresses in each slot in the daily lesson. Each shift calls for the teacher to adjust her planning, her expectations and her interactions with the learner.

CHANGES WITHIN THE LESSON OVER AN INDIVIDUAL PROGRAMME

1   Rereading familiar books

I   Attention to concepts, direction and space-time links of print and speech.
II   Orchestrating all the moves on continuous text to achieve effective reading.
III   Word and part-word processing embedded in text reading on the run.

2   Rereading yesterday's new book

I, II, and III above all applied to new books.

3   Letter identification and making and breaking

I   Mostly learning to identify letters by some means.
A little making and breaking of words but only those already known.
II   Use of making and breaking using onsets and rimes, and analogy.
III   As in II but embedded within words (and occurring while the child is reading text).

4   Writing a story

I   Creating texts, working on direction, learning letters, hearing sounds in words, monitoring all aspects of the task.
II   Word-making, how to expand writing vocabulary, gaining more control.
III   Independent work with creating texts and making words.

5   Hearing and recording sounds in words

I   Gets some phonemes, any position.
II   Gets consonants, and in left-to-right order, and most letters with some independence.
III   Gets most words by independent analysis using phonological and orthographic knowledge.

6   Cut-up story

I   Monitors by a few features in the print.
II   Controls direction, initiates checking, notes errors and corrects.
III   Completed at times for practice, but by now there is not a lot of novel learning to be done.

7   Introduction to the new book

I   Orientation to the story and preparing the child to remember to use his strengths or new learning, plus emphasis on one or two new things to be learned.
II   Orientation and help with particular difficulties of the child's processing.
III   A more summary overview leaving much more for the child to discover while reading.

8   New book attempted

I   Applying what is known to new text, with assistance, and teaching after story is complete but only on selected important items.
II   Still assisted with prompting and priming, and telling if need be but more a practice session for reading novel text.
III   Teacher is looking for a smoothly operating reading system that is self-extending. She is still helpful.

4 | READING RECOVERY TEACHING PROCEDURES

INTRODUCTION

These teaching procedures were developed with children who had been at school for one year and who were unable to make satisfactory progress in their classrooms. It is unnecessary to teach most children in these ways.

The procedures are arranged so that a teacher can turn to the approach she requires for a particular child with a particular problem. Many of the suggestions that are detailed will not be appropriate for some children. As these procedures were being developed over a three-year period we became convinced that the difficulties which children have in learning to read differ markedly from child to child (see Reading Recovery Research Reports pages 60–97). *The teacher must skilfully select the activities needed by a particular child.* Otherwise she will slow the child's progress further by having him complete unnecessary work, thereby wasting precious learning time.

If the teacher is to respond to individual differences she cannot begin with the Early Learning sections and then move to Intermediate sections and then to the Advanced Learning sections. For a particular child the teacher will need to work at different levels across many of the procedures and perhaps even look up a particular problem or two as well.

The hard-to-teach children who need this early intervention do not follow predictable paths of progress. That is why individually delivered and individually designed teaching is needed.

And if the teacher begins to expect certain competencies to emerge before others she is forcing a sequence of change on the child when the essential feature of this programme is that teachers remain responsive to leaps forward, or confusions and regressions that emerge during the teaching of a particular child.

1 LEARNING ABOUT DIRECTION

Introduction

In my studies I have found that learning about direction can be very confusing for young children. Some directional confusions may be found in all beginning readers who are learning the arbitrary rules we use to write down languages. Such confusions persist for some children who are having difficulty in learning to read (see Clay, 1991a).

Children who have poor motor coordination, and those who are quick and impulsive, and those who are timid and do not like to try a new task may experience directional problems and will require more time than usual and sensitive teaching to establish directional behaviour. Another small group of children who need help are those who have learned and practised peculiar directional habits for a long time.

There is more to this than just learning how to move across a line of print. What the learner has to do early in his exploration of literacy is begin to attend to print in ways that are consistent with the serial order rules of the written language (Clay, 1991a). Watching a parent reading a familiar story book the preschool child may catch on to the movement across a line of print, and the turning of the book pages, and the learner may begin attending to print according to the right serial order rules for English. There are several concepts or movements to put in place, however, such as

- left page before a right page
- top of the page downwards
- left to right across a line
- return sweep to the left of the next line
- left to right across a word
- the use one can make of spaces
- and what is '*the first letter*'.

Simple yet complex. The teacher can help the child to work in this way without direct teaching and without verbal direction, but with some demonstration, and with careful monitoring.

Avoid talk about direction

For a few children, and only as a temporary device, it may be necessary for the child to guide his own movement with words that remind him of what to do. This must be unlearned later because the movement pattern must become a habit that is used automatically without requiring the child to attend to it.

So, avoid talking about these action patterns if possible. Model the action for the child as often as he needs this help.

Recording procedures

Directional behaviour is complex to record when it does not follow the rules of written language. A set of simple procedures for recording it are outlined. They have helped teachers to record what children actually do when they are just learning about direction and print.

Record the child's directional responses to the print in a book with simple text. Ask the child to 'Read it with your finger'. Record any lapse from correct responding.

- Show the horizontal direction with arrows ——▶ ——▶
- Show the vertical direction by numbering the lines

    (3) ————————▶

    (2) ————————▶

    (1) ————————▶

- Show whether the page was a left or right one (Lp/Rp).
- Show whether the child used a left or right hand (Lh/Rh).

A sample record from one child not yet controlling directional behaviour might look like this:

Teacher's record   **Position on page**

Page 1
  (1) ——▶ $\frac{Lp}{Lh}$ This would mean correct direction on a left page pointing with the left hand.

Page 2
  (1) ⟋——▶ $\frac{Rp}{Rh}$ On a right page with the right hand the child moved from right to left and back on the next line from left to right.

Page 3
  (2) ◀—— $\frac{Rp}{Rh}$ On a right page with the right hand the child moved from right to left and from bottom to top.

Page 4
  ◀—— $\frac{Lp}{Lh}$ On a left page with the left hand the child moved from right to left and from left to right.

The (tentative) interpretation of this record might be:

- that the child had learned very little about the directional rules of print
- that he used his left hand on a left page and his right hand on a right page
- that a starting position at the top left of a page had not been established
- that top to bottom direction was not consistent.

Recovery procedures

The teacher must give clear demonstrations with few words. She must give praise and positive reinforcement for any attempts that are close to what is required.

Starting position

Check each new book introduced to the child to see that the starting position on a page will not confuse this particular child.

- Accept either hand, whichever he chooses to use.
- Control the directional behaviour by pointing to the starting position on the page or line.
- Provide opportunities for overlearning (that means practice well beyond the point where you think the behaviour is learned).
- Prevent the child from starting in the wrong place by various devices, such as intercepting a false move and gently bringing the child's hand to the correct position.

Starting signal

Where the child moves incorrectly across print a signal such as a green sticker (green light for Go) can be used to indicate the starting point to the left of the text.

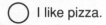 I like pizza.

The child's working space may need this signal also. So be prepared to use it:

- on the blackboard
- on the table top
- on paper.

Some teachers are surprised when they find that a child who controls direction in one place uses different directional responses in another place.

To assist orientation on more complex text a coloured line or margin can be placed on the left side of the page.

    | I like pizza
    | and ice cream
    | and coke.

A helping hand

Teachers should not be afraid to encourage hand action to assist reading.

For the most difficult cases, passively move the child's hand and arm through the appropriate movements until he can manage without this guidance.

The child's pointing finger will guide his directional behaviour as it becomes more stable in:

- establishing a top left starting point
- consistent left to right movement across lines
- matching words in speech to words in text, one after the other
- locating the first letter of lines
- locating the first letter of words.

A clear pointing finger (rather than a vague cluster of fingers) seems to help most.

Do away with signals

The child should do away with signals like stickers and margin lines as soon as he has gained some control over the top left starting position.

Do away with the helping hand

If finger pointing is allowed to persist it may become a prop which gets in the way of fluent reading. So as correct directional responding becomes more consistent the teacher can begin to discourage pointing with the finger. This has been an aid to having the eyes and brain attend to words in the text. Voice pointing (Clay, 1991a) will often be heard, telling you that the reader is still attending word by word. Before long the teacher can begin to require the child to read groups of words together, using the phrasing that is natural in normal speech, and the intonation of normal conversation. When this is stressed the child will drop the finger pointing (with strong encouragement to do this if necessary). It is appropriate for the learner to return to using hand support

- when a text is new and difficult
- when he is tired
- when the layout is unusual
- when he is incorporating some new aspect of behaviour into his established system of reading behaviour.

Choice of texts

In the early stages of learning about direction the child will be helped by the use of texts in which the layout is similar and the text begins towards the top left of the page. As the child gains control over direction more variable layout should be introduced to ensure that he becomes flexible in his approach to print. Aim for stable control over direction before you push for flexibility.

The end goal

The goal is a particular movement pattern suited to books, blackboards, paper and almost all print. It has probably been achieved when the child

- can use either hand to point to print
- on either page
- without lapse in direction
- or with self-correction following a lapse.

Different children will reach this end-goal in different ways. Most (but not all) will use an index finger and most will prefer to use a particular hand for a period before the flexibility of the end-goal is reached (Clay, 1982).

Once the movement pattern is established pointing will not be needed but the movement pattern guides eye movements in reading, a very important outcome.

2 LOCATING RESPONSES

Introduction

Young children have difficulty pointing to a row of objects in sequence one after the other. This has been accepted as important in early mathematics lessons but few have noted that this is also a limitation for reading. It may mean that the child cannot attend to one printed word at a time in sequential order.

Most school entrants can do this or will quickly learn to do this in the first year at school. A few children having difficulty with learning to read will need special help in learning these responses.

Ask a child to point to each word in a simple one-line text. If he fails to do this there may be several reasons. Only one reason is considered here; he cannot *attend to*, *focus on* or *point to* one word after the other.

Use some activities like those that follow to establish these behaviours.

Recovery procedures

Early learning

One after the other put down two objects in a row. Call the child's attention to them and point to them one after the other, the left one first. *Don't count them.*

Ask the child to *point* to a row of three objects; four objects; five objects or more; in sequence one after the other. Record:

- the starting point
- the direction
- any difficulties.

Intermediate steps

Repeat the task with objects and sequences like felt dots, geometric shapes, pencil dots, two-letter words (same and different), five-word sentences. *It is probably wise to avoid using single letters*. Record:

- the starting point
- the direction
- any difficulties.

Provide practice, using the appropriate directional pattern for print.

The goal is coordinated, one-to-one correspondence with the movement pattern needed for print and pointing to individual symbols in a set.

Now ask the child to tell you about the objects in sequence. Without pointing:

- name the objects
- name the colour of the dots
- give the number of dots.

Advanced learning

Words and spaces on books with:

- one line per page
- two lines per page
- more than two lines.

If the child needs help to *see* the words and spaces between words write out a line or two of the text of the book in large print exaggerating the spaces.

Cut the sentence up into single words as the child watches. Get the child to remake the sentence and reread it several times, pointing carefully.

You can rearrange the cut-out words with *overempha-sised spaces at first*, gradually reducing these to normal spacing. To develop an accurate locating response on book texts for the child who still has difficulties:

- Use two-finger framing (with two index fingers).
- Use a long pointer. (It requires more effort to control the movement.)
- Encourage deliberate voice pointing.

The extra control needed to accomplish these more difficult motor tasks slows down speech so that the child feels the pauses between the spoken words while his fingers show the boundaries of the written words.

Work for flexibility

Once a good locating response has been established on a familiar book with two-finger framing get the child to read with one-finger pointing.

If you are using cut-up stories (the child's stories that are written out and cut up) these can be rearranged by the teacher in several ways—one line, two lines, three lines, to foster this flexibility:

- I went to the zoo.

- I went
  to the zoo.

- I went
  to the
  zoo.

Take the opportunity to ask the child to read a few words of the story on each rearrangement. As a more advanced task cut-up stories can be rearranged *by the child*. The teacher alters the size of the space in which the child is asked to remake the story:

- larger   I   am   a   big   girl

- progressively smaller   I am a
                            big girl

The children who have most difficulty with learning about direction tend to have problems with this type of task.

Too many breaks

Over-segmenting can cause difficulties with one-to-one correspondence. For example:

A	way	we	go
Away	we	go	to

To overcome a bad case of too many breaks exaggerate the segments with magnetic letters spatially and also with shouting or singing, then gradually rejoin the two segments again.

A—way
Away

Caution

For most children the activities described in this section will be unnecessary. They learn these things incidentally while exploring books in a more enjoyable way.

There is no point in delaying a child's progress with such a detailed programme unless these activities have value for a particular problem that has not responded to other approaches.

3   SPATIAL LAYOUT

Introduction

In trying to write stories some children have become very confused about how to use the space on the page. Sometimes this also involves confused concepts of the relationships of letters to words. The following activities may help if the child shows confusion.

Recovery procedures

Arranging letters in words

• After letter identification work in any lesson (or at other opportune times) use *magnetic letters* to build letters into words that are already known. Exaggerate the space between letters in some well known words and get the child to return them to the normal spacing. Pull them apart and bring them together.

Arranging words in texts

• Use *magnetic letters* to make words into a short phrase or sentence. Then accentuate the spaces between words and get the child to return them to normal spacing.

In writing

• Help the child to leave a finger space between words, saying 'It is easier for us to read'.
• With little comment help the child to use the space on the page appropriately in spacing his sentences. This help might mean pointing to a definite starting position—top left-hand corner, indicating 'the way to go' or when and where to start a new line, or anticipating for the child when a word will be too big for the space available. The child will learn from this help how to organise his text on the page, without much direct instruction.

In cut-up stories

• The child will also learn about space in cut-up stories. Help the child to remake the story several times, each time altering the space in which he is working so that he is forced to reorganise the layout of the story to fit the 'spatial frame' which you have created by your use of the table top.

The aim in these activities is to give the child the ability to organise himself in relation to written language space. *Therefore, any aids and props should be used only for the period for which they are essential.*

An important note   We have not found lined paper a help for story writing. It makes too many demands on the child who has difficulty with spatial learning or with confusions. It does not allow the teacher to take the child from where he is but suddenly it imposes many constraints on his performance that he is not yet ready for. The teacher may add cues and prompts to the blank unlined paper if these seem to help—only for a short time, though. Then the child should learn to work without them. The child who gradually learns to organise his production within the conventions of the printer's code on blank pages transfers easily to lined paper.

4   LEARNING TO LOOK AT PRINT

Introduction

The eye does not photograph the detail of print and transfer it to the brain. The child must learn to attend to the details in print respecting the rules of direction, the order or sequences of letters, and the order of words. Some children, finding this difficult or tedious, coast along on their language skills and pay as little attention to the detail of print as they can get away with.

Theorists may argue over whether readers look at all the print detail or only sample some of it. However, the beginning reader can only sample some features in print which he recognises. Gradually he must learn how to pay attention to different kinds of information in print (different types of cues) so that he can do this when it is necessary to do so. A child who only knows a few letters and words is probably not using many visual signposts or cues. Ways of looking at print and searching for cues must be established. *Most children will discover all that they need to know as they read books.* A few children take a very passive approach to print. They need more help in learning about print.

Many teachers who think of reading and writing as language activities find it difficult to think about what children are looking at when they look at print. What signals in the print are the children attending to? Sometimes we can see in their writing the answer to a question like that. Sometimes what they say tells us what they are looking at. Most of the time we really do not know what the early reader is attending to in print.

What the child did on the Observation Survey tasks provides the teacher with some hypotheses. Refer to the Concepts About Print task (Clay, 1993) which highlights visual survey of direction, and the changed order of letters in words provides hints as to whether the child pays attention to word order, to first or last letters, or to letter order within words. When a child confuses the concepts of 'a letter' and 'a word' in the final items on that task this is a warning to the teacher that the child may not be able to attend to the first letter of a word. Other Observation Survey tasks can be scanned with this question in mind: 'What is the child attending to as he looks at print on the page?'

For Reading Recovery children it is advisable to let them attend to what is easy for them and work from there, rather than have a preconceived sequence of visual attention learning in mind. It is necessary to be alert at all times to what the children are directing their attention to.

Recovery procedures

Early learning
At an early stage in the programme the teacher helps the child to gain footholds in print: the child learns some letters and some simple words to begin to work with.

Looking at print
Start from the known and move out very slowly to anything new. Children who know few letters will usually differentiate new letters very slowly.

When the child begins lessons the 'known' may be not more than:

- the child's name
- a few words which he can read and/or write
- one or two particular books
- the child's dictated stories.

From the focus of the child's vocabulary the teaching can slowly move towards extending the child on each activity above.

Here is a first lesson in a recovery programme built around the child's name. The teacher uses three ways of directing the child's attention to visual features of print.

- The teacher says '*Make your name here*,' but the child makes no response. The teacher begins to write the child's name.
- She pays attention to the first letter, saying '*We make it like this*.'
- She models the movements vertically in the air.

The teacher works on *three ways of remembering*.

1	Movement	The teacher holds the child's hand and guides him. This identifies the letters by *movement*.
2	Words	'*Down and around*', she says. This is a *verbal* description of movement.
3	Visual form	She writes the letter in his book. This is a *visual* model. (She may ask the child to write it also.)

The teacher writes the rest of the child's name and he copies this. From this the child learns

- some specific letters
- how to put them in a set sequence
- several features of letters, usable in other letters
- several features of words.

Suggestions for extending a knowledge of letters
The child should be developing new knowledge in many aspects of reading and writing at the same time. He will be learning new things about story texts, new concepts about print, new words, and letters or clusters of letters. The fact that this section begins with a focus on letters does not mean that this should be the focus of all teaching. The child can begin to read words with only a limited knowledge of letters; he can read text with only a limited knowledge of words.

This section on letter learning is merely for the convenience of the novice Reading Recovery teacher. What is discussed occurs in one short segment of a lesson. Many whole-text and whole-word activities precede and follow the letter work in every lesson.

What to do with magnetic letters
Magnetic letters are colourful and three-dimensional, and so they lend themselves to feel and to movement.

Movement   The movement of letters can begin large and bold, and become minimal. The movement can also be demonstrated by the teacher in deliberate ways as if to stress particular points in the construction process. The child can group and regroup letters. Teachers need a large clear magnetic board placed so that the child can stand in front of it and move the letters easily.

Production   The child can build, dismember, and rebuild small collections of letters several times, and quickly. Pairing and grouping are good activities. Writing is a slower process. The producing of one or two words, which are also dismembered and rebuilt, aids the child's visual discrimination of letters, as well as a vague understanding of the ways in which letters come together to make words.

Variation   Varied positions, sizes, and means of making letters help the child to achieve a knowledge of the constant features and at the same time help to avoid the child making an unimportant feature his main signal.

What makes this easy?

At first use only the letters the child can already identify. Give him lots of practice with these. Introduce new letters into an array of letters the child already knows.

Add easy-to-see letters first.

Letters will be easier to identify in isolation and hard when embedded within words or within continuous text.

However children need, in the long run, to see and recognise letters in all these settings.

As the child works with letters:

- allow the child to label letters in *any* appropriate way—by name, by sound, or by word beginning. We find good readers use all three ways of identifying letters. It seems to be useful to have more than one way of labelling a letter, and we suggest that you do not insist on only one type of label being used.
- have the child run over the new letter with his finger to feel the shape. Identify the letter by name. Talk about the similarity/dissimilarity of the capital and lower-case forms.
- model the formation of the new letter with chalk on the blackboard, writing in large print and directing the movements verbally.
- give him verbal instructions, and guide his hand if necessary. Have the child write the letter
  - — in the air
  - — on the blackboard
  - — in sand.

Teachers in our programme developed many interesting activities for drawing children's attention to the features of letters, such as sticky coloured paper cut-outs, formation cards showing where to start letters, tracing paper activities, and so on.

Only do what is essential. Do not get too focused on letters.

Things to do with similarities

- Introduce seeing similarities on letters the child knows.
- Match, pair or group similar letters using only lower case.
- Ask the child to find the odd one in a group (a harder task).

Things to do with differences

- Introduce the activity on letters the child knows.
- Contrast the most different first.

Things to do with arbitrary categories

- Learn capital and lower-case pairs.

Things to do with variation

- Sort the same letters in different colours.
- Sort different letters in the same colours.
- Pair capital and lower-case letters in different colours.

Work for flexibility

- Use vertical and horizontal surfaces.
- Use different mediums—felt pen, chalk, magnetic letters.
- For a particular child use unusual mediums—sandpaper or felt letters.
- Use different sizes of print.
- Look for a *simple* book that illustrates the new letter and read through it, having the child find examples of the letter in the text.
- Get the child to identify the new letter by an object which he identifies with it.
- Go through his alphabet book (see page 26) to show him where the new letter fits in sequence and draw the key picture and the letter forms.
- If appropriate teach a new word starting with that letter.

Every new thing learned should be revised in several other activities.

Extending the knowledge of letters aims to have the child give some identity to each of the letter forms. Be cautious with published materials which seem to be helpful. Most have been constructed with another, and different aim—to have the children learn a sound for every letter symbol.

It is not the aim of Reading Recovery to have the child learn a sound for every letter symbol but rather to learn that in English sometimes a letter has one sound and in other contexts it can have a different sound. This means that the child must have in mind choosing which of several possible sounds this particular letter may have.

For consistency always do a little letter work after taking the Running Record in the lesson. When most of the letters are known shift to some speedy work on making and breaking words and give attention to generating new words from known words (Section 10, page 43).

When children confuse letters

Some children have well-established habits of confusing letters. One way to help them control and monitor these unwanted responses on the one hand, and develop desirable new responses on the other, is to bring the behaviour under verbal direction for a short time. This practice must be used sensitively. It is a temporary device which if continued for too long will itself become an unwanted response, slowing up the fast responding required.

- Attend to similarities and differences of letters.
- Use three-dimensional forms such as magnetic letters and create clear demonstrations of any distinctions that the child should learn.
- Put three or four examples of the same letter onto the magnetic board. Jumble the forms with some known letters and have the child find 'all the Es' and put them in a line.

Because it takes Reading Recovery children some time to distinguish letters revise new learning frequently. As they become very familiar with some letters those letters can be omitted from the practice exercises.

Attend to the forming of letters which are confused

Draw the child a model on the blackboard slowly, directing the movements verbally. Ask the child to try, and guide his hand if necessary. Verbalise the movement (*'Make k down, and in and out'*). Try to bring the child's movements under your verbal control and then transfer this verbal control to the child. Continue to practise after the child gives the correct response and revise often. Attend to letter formation only if it is essential, and only to one or two letters at any one time.

Attend to common faults

The child sometimes adopts an awkward starting position, for example. If this is important direct attention to it. Be firm about essentials, that is, whatever your most important teaching points are, and ignore other inadequacies. You cannot afford to overteach on non-essentials. It costs too much in motivation.

Letter names

You may direct the child's attention to movement or to visual shape. But if you want to talk about the letters it usually helps to use letter names. They seem to act as a shorthand type of label representing many other experiences with letters.

Three important points

Letter learning for most children is done incidentally as they learn to read stories but special help with letter learning is needed for Reading Recovery children. It should always be a *minor part* of a recovery programme. The child cannot afford to waste time on letter learning activities or games when he could be reading well-chosen books. Careful judgement is needed to give the child just enough opportunity to gain control of letter identification.

In many cases of letter confusion an appropriate strategy is to help the child gain control of *one* of the confusing letters before introducing the second. *It does not help most children to work on confusable letters side by side.*

The aim is to have a child recognise letters as rapidly as we do without any props. He needs to end up with a fast recognition response. Be careful to arrange your teaching so that it leads to this.

An alphabet book

Early learning

It is usually desirable to take stock of and tidy up a child's knowledge of the alphabet. One idea that works well with children having difficulty is to make a paper book which will allow the alphabet to be printed in sequence, with a drawing for each letter the child knows. Use the form of the letter that the child already knows, capital or lower case.

When a child knows more than 10 letters write *these letters only* in the alphabet book leaving gaps for letters yet to be learned. Use a key picture which the child himself identifies with that letter already.

The child has a feel for the size of the task, how far he has gone, what he knows for certain and as the letters not yet known are flipped over, he must feel that it is important to be sure of and use what he knows and to overlook, for the present, some of the difficulties.

The child's own alphabet book has proved more useful than published books we have tried. Yet for the child having little difficulty with reading, a beautifully illustrated alphabet book would be an enriching experience.

Advanced learning of the alphabet

When the child has fairly extensive control over letter knowledge practise sequencing the alphabet by getting him to give the consecutive letter before you turn to that page. In the next example the teacher has one letter only on each double page opening.

Teacher (pointing):   a—apple
Child (anticipating):   *b—balloon*
                       (Turn the page)

Teacher (pointing):   c—cat
Child (anticipating):   *d—dog*
                       (Turn the page)

Avoid saying *'a is for apple'* because many children try to find a printed sign for *is for*.

What contribution does knowing the letter names make?

- Firstly, it is very helpful to have a way of talking about these small units of print—this level of print organisation—providing a metalanguage for talking about printed forms, in reading or writing.
- Secondly, the whole alphabet has very little use except that it provides the child with a record, or collection, or inventory of the reference points to which he can anchor his current efforts.
- Thirdly, it provides the detail of the journey taken and a map of the length of journey yet to be taken.

Suggestions for extending a meagre knowledge of words

At this time the child is also learning to look at his first words. He knows so few words that we need to think of words he can read and words he can write as the pool of his knowledge about words. A glimmer of recognition in either reading or in writing is a beginning out of which knowledge of the word can emerge through many contacts in different settings.

Because Reading Recovery children have small repertoires of responding to print any letter work or word work should arise from the texts they are working on, in reading or in writing. The same new things should pop up in different contexts. It is most unhelpful for the child of limited repertoire to have new things in the new book, different new things in letter identification work, more new things in writing, and another novel surprise in the cut-up story. What letters and words the teacher chooses to work with should, to some extent, be linked across activities. There are echoes from one part of the lesson to another part, echoes which the learner can discover for himself. The child can learn how to find what he knows in different places which is helpful when he only has a small repertoire of responding.

Many of the new words in reading will be acquired through reading books, and through a carryover from the daily writing. Gradually the new reader will come to notice more and more of the visual features of the print he is reading and writing.

In these procedures children work on words in several components of the lesson.

- From working with the child in reading text the teacher decides which words are the ones she would like this child to give more attention to as he reads texts.
- One way of remembering a word in all its detail is to be able to write it. This requires one to have learned a little program (like a computer program) which produces the word from beginning to end, with all its parts in the right order.
- Making words with magnetic letters and breaking them up to form new words seems to model the construction of the word for the child.

Some of the things that may help a child learn to read and write a new word are these.

- Make a word out of magnetic letters as the child watches. Jumble it and have the child remake it, perhaps more than once.
- Write the word in big print as the child watches you.
- Ask the child to trace the word with finger contact saying each part of the word as he traces it.
- Use a paint-brush and water to make a disappearing word on the blackboard.
- Use wet chalk to make a magic 'appearing' word on the blackboard.
- Ask the child to construct/write the word many times getting fluency and overlearning.

Keep these words in mind to use in other activities. At the same time teachers will be gradually extending the child's writing vocabulary. A useful initial vocabulary can be selected from:

Child's name, I, a, is, in, am, to, come, like, see, the, my, we, and, at, here, on, up, look, go, this, it, me.

These words help with the stories the child tries to write and with the first books he can read. Try to keep all words within the vocabulary that he controls, and slowly add to this.

Reading Recovery teachers have found it useful to build up vocabulary charts for individual children, to be read, referred to, and added to during lessons (see also Section 5, page 28).

Another idea is to build up a box of word cards indexed by letters of the alphabet. Such a *collection of partly-known words* has several uses.

- It provides a child-sized concept of what he is trying to master (just as the alphabet book does for letters).
- It helps him to remember a word, that is, it is a retrieval device.
- It reminds the teacher of earlier work the child has done. Known words and words that prove unmanageable can be withdrawn (discreetly) from the collection.

5   WRITING STORIES

Introduction

Many of the operations needed in early reading are practised in another form in early writing (see page 10). The focus of this section is on getting the child to compose and write his own stories. It is also about *constructing words from their parts*. This is not a matter of copying words and stories: it concerns

- going from ideas
- to spoken words
- to printed messages
- and rereading those messages.

First lessons in a Reading Recovery programme will have explored what letters and words the child can already write. The number of letters he knows should be expanded as quickly as letter learning will allow. (See Learning to Look at Print, page 23.)

The Hearing and Recording Sounds in Words analysis and making and breaking words using magnetic letters are also supportive activities for early writing. These should be concurrent activities (see pages 32 and 43).

The writing down of the child's orally composed messages can be shared by the teacher and child in interaction from the early learning stage. The learner is expected to write all that he can independently, but the teacher writes more at the beginning and the child takes over more and more of the task until little teacher help is required.

Calling these sentences 'stories' seems to teachers too pretentious for the very short messages which the lowest achievers tend to produce in the short time allocated during a Reading Recovery lesson. Some children struggle to compose orally even the briefest message. Yet during the course of a recovery programme a low achiever learns to bring together:

- the ideas
- the composing of the message (which must be his own)
- the search for ways to record it
- the monitoring of the message production
- the reading of the record made.

When the child is at the end of his programme he will have fluent control of these practical aspects of story production and will be ready to blossom into producing stories of greater length and quality back in his classroom programme.

Recovery procedures

For these stories Reading Recovery teachers use unlined exercise books (the size of commercial letter paper), turned sideways. There is a working space for teacher and child to use in the top half, as they discuss, problem-solve, and construct together. The teacher links up what the child already knows with what he is now trying to do. The child writes the story on the bottom page.

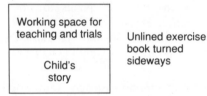

Story production is a shared activity between child and teacher. In the working space on the top page the child may try out a word that he thinks he knows, or an analysis of hearing the sequence of sounds in a word may be carried out, or sometimes the child will be asked to do repeated writings of particular high-frequency or high-utility words (see page 30). The teacher can write models of letters or words which the child may copy into his story. This working page provides a record of most of the teacher-child interaction about any aspect of the writing.

Before writing

The child can be invited to reread one or more of his previous stories. This will be familiar text, written in 'correct form', and indicates the value placed on writing and the messages in writing.

The child composes a story

The child is invited to tell a story, following the procedure outlined below. (Early in the programme this 'story' will be a message in a sentence, and when he can write more it may be two or three sentences.) It can be about anything he wants to write about—some experience he has had, a message to someone, *something that interests him*. The important thing is that he must compose the message and feel he 'owns' it.

First *talk with the child*. Guided by what you know of the child start up a conversation about things like

- something he has done
- a story he has heard or read
- a TV programme he has seen
- something that interests him
- an experience you have had together
- a book he enjoyed reading
- the best part of a story he has just read.

Arising from this genuine but short conversation, and at an appropriate point when the child shows he has something to say, you might shift to an invitation like 'What could you write about that?' Vary this invitation to compose, otherwise it becomes merely a signal that he is now going to write, like it or not! Encourage him to tell you his story (sentence). Draw it out of the reluctant composers. Repeat the child's story, showing interest, while you scribble down the sentence for your own reference. Perhaps the child can repeat the sentence (often they cannot!) but a request for the child to do this often sounds to him like a rejection of what he said, and he will alter it. Thinking about this the teacher may still want the child to repeat the sentence so that he has it clearly in his head, something against which to monitor his own writing.

We want the child to have a clear memory of the sentence he composed, because he will monitor his writing production against the remembered sentence. Sometimes you may want to help the child to word the sentence so that it contains words he can write, but do this very rarely.

If the teacher alters the child's sentence he is very likely to become confused and to not remember her alteration. The process of composing (for writing) is at a delicate stage of formation and is thrown by interference of this kind. Sometimes you may encourage him to expand on his statement.

There may be time in the earlier lessons for the child to draw a picture about his story, but very soon, to save time, this activity must be omitted as the child's writing confidence grows. Provide thin felt pens, pencils or ballpoint pens for him to choose from.

The child writes

The writing can occur in three ways:

1 the child writes what he can independently

2 the teacher writes into the story what she judges to be too hard for the child to attempt at this stage of his learning, sharing the task

3 the teacher and child work together on words at the cutting edge of his learning, interacting in a variety of ways, and making good use of the working page.

So this is a co-construction task with many teaching interactions occurring.

Always encourage the child to write as much as he can alone each session. Encourage him to write the words you think he might know. Praise him for his efforts. The child may write the words he thinks he knows on his practice page first, if he needs to check on himself. The teacher may write some of the easier words on the practice page for him to copy or she may write the difficult words into the story for him. (Copying the teacher's model is not a good way to help the child because it does not reinforce the 'construction' of the word as an important process to be learned.)

The teacher's role and her ways of interacting should change as the child moves through the programme. (*This is true in all programme procedures.*)

1 In the early lessons the teacher's contribution to the production is high because she is creating the opportunities for the child to do what he can, write what he knows, and learn something new. For example, when the child comes to a problem word the teacher can help him to attend to and isolate at least the initial sound and predict what he would expect to see at the beginning. She may get him to write the first letter and then write the rest of the word for him.

2 There should be a gradual takeover by the child as writer and the teacher's contribution should change—to reminding, prompting, and facilitating the production by the child. The sound analysis techniques described in the next section (Section 6) will be used a great deal when it is judged that the word he needs to write is a word he may easily learn to analyse at this stage of his programme.

3 Towards the end of a child's programme the teacher's role shifts to monitoring the child's performance, anticipating any problem-solving difficulties, and teaching more by talking than by demonstration.

Activities like those described in Section 10, page 43 can be introduced momentarily while the child is writing stories, if this is occasionally helpful.

To get fluent writing

When the child works on a high-frequency word (the little words that occur very frequently in the language) on the working page and you would like him to know it the next time he needs to write it, say some of the following: *'Do it again. And again. Now write it here. And here. Do it faster. Once more. Come and write it on the board. Use the magnetic letters.'* This procedure helps the child to practise producing the *sequence* of letters needed for that word, and to do this with a minimum of attention. It is like having a little movement programme for producing that word.

- This builds fluency in constructing the word.
- It helps the child to remember the word in every detail.

Come back to this word again next day, or for several days, asking each time for the same fluent writing. Take a few seconds at the beginning or end of a lesson to review the most recent words you have taken to fluency, providing help if necessary.

To get flexibility

Over time try to get flexibility by having the child construct the word in different places with a variety of materials—with magnetic letters, with chalk, with his finger on the desk, or water and a paintbrush on a board, on a wipeout board or with felt pen.

Which words would the teacher choose?

The easy-to-write words which occur often in all sentences scaffold the sentence leaving the writer's attention free to work on new challenges. Choose

- words with a high utility
- words which occur most often in the language
- words needed often in writing
- words the child almost knows that a little more practice will bring to overlearning.

When the child has a useful knowledge of high-frequency words then a word might be selected because its spelling pattern could lead the writer, by analogy, to other similar words.

Be careful not to choose words because they fit your personal ideas about word families and phonological similarities. The words should have value in getting acceleration for this particular child, given his current knowledge.

Later in the programme

The teacher's role changes as the child becomes more adept at writing his stories. There is less need to do as much work on the work page. The writer knows when he can write a new word without boxes, and the teacher may feel there is little need to trial the word on the work page. However, she still needs to interact with the learner and does this orally. Some of the following things may be appropriate.

- When he comes to a problem word help him to attend to and isolate the initial sound or cluster and write it.
- Have him predict what else he would expect to see (and accept out-of-sequence components).
- Tell him the hard bits, often the vowels, if this will avoid creating confusions.
- If necessary write the word for him to copy.

Notice that what the teacher used to have to put down on the work page can now often be done through talking. But do not give up demonstration altogether.

Errors in written stories

One way to approach writing and spelling errors is to know the learner so well that you anticipate a child's difficulty and offer help before errors occur. The teacher should be alert to the possible occurrence of old error patterns and try to intervene before the old habit is allowed to take over. If the teacher's attention has shifted to her record-keeping the child may quickly produce old errors: teachers must be watching the production of the writing in order to intervene to prevent old errors from occurring.

Another approach is to allow the child to stop when he recognises that something has gone wrong, because he is monitoring his own work. If the child is too quick for you and the error is already on the page mask the error in some way (white stick-on labels for example) and then help the child to construct a correct attempt by some interaction on the work page.

The visual analysis of words into useful letter clusters will also be developed in writing and so will sound-to-letter analyses. The child will want to hurriedly write down the clusters he knows, resisting a teacher's attempts to get him to work letter by letter. And rightly so. But intercept a too hasty response, calling for the child to demonstrate control over the contemplated activity, saying 'Try it on your practice page', 'Show how it would start', 'Tell me what you would write' or some such call to have the child attend to the detail of what he is doing.

Rereading

Get the child to reread the story. At first he will need to point word by word, and the teacher may need to reread his story with him. Before long the completed story is something the child can read independently, monitoring the reading against his inner knowledge of what he intended to write.

Type out the story

Sometimes it is appropriate to type out whatever the child writes and have him read it before too long an interval. (Children sometimes like to have printed copies of their stories.) Computer printout facilities may be used. Larger type with generous spacing is a particular help to some children. DO NOT use capital letters to solve the type-size problem.

In this resetting of the child's story resist the urge to edit or elaborate it. Change as little of the child's story as is consistent with good teaching. Paste this typed version into the child's unlined exercise book for revision reading.

Records of words written independently

Prepare a list of the child's known words from the Writing Vocabulary test as a guide to what you can ask the child to write independently in his early stories.

Make a record each week of the new words the child can write without your help, as the child learns them (see page 104).

The following format has been found useful as a record of the build-up of writing vocabulary.

Initial Testing	Wk 1	2	3	4	5	6	7
Name is	the a	I at my	on and me	she in	home do	he	
2	4	7	10	12	14	15	

Keeping a cumulative total

If you total the weekly words under the list, adding them cumulatively, these numbers can be plotted on a Writing Progress graph which records the accumulated writing vocabulary that the teacher believes, from her observations in lessons, the child can write independently (see Clay, 1993).

Observable changes in sentence writing

A Reading Recovery programme lasts on average only about 12 to 15 weeks but during this time many changes occur in children's control over writing. Each change in the child's control calls for an adjustment in what the teacher does. It is not possible to describe the infinite range of ways in which a teacher might work with individual children but the following list of changes that have been observed as children make progress in the programme is provided as a reminder to teachers of how and when they might change the direction and emphasis in their teaching.

Consistent with a major principle in Reading Recovery the emphasis is on children's strengths and what they can do. The observant teacher may note that the learner

- can control more and more high-frequency words
- shifts from laborious writing of known words to fluent production

- can hear sounds but cannot write them
- can hear and record some dominant consonants
- can hear and record first and last consonants
- can hear and record some vowels
- gets more of the consonant framework

- uses what he knows about letters and words in response to the teacher's prompt to work on a new word
- sees the relationship of a word he wants to write with something he has already written
- initiates use of what he knows about letters and words to get to a new word

- is comfortable with the use of silent letters, particularly silent *e*
- adds inflections without having to work on them
- uses analogies or spelling patterns quite deliberately

- needs less teacher help on the words he has to work on
- can write an increasing proportion of words independently
- is gaining a good control of the spelling combinations of English vowels
- writes increasingly long and complex sentences, as if this is a challenge.

For some children

- shifts occur in the use of space and the size of print
- there is an increase in legibility.

There is a lot to be learned about writing down a language and later changes are dependent upon the sound foundation created by earlier changes.

6 HEARING AND RECORDING SOUNDS IN WORDS

Introduction

These activities are designed to help the child think about the order of sounds in spoken words, and to help the child to analyse a new word he wants to write into its sequence of sounds. The activities are included in the writing lesson, and the teacher chooses from the story the child has composed two or three words they can profitably work on together.

These 'writing' activities have an important relationship with progress in reading. The beginning reader of stories anticipates 'upcoming words' from his semantic and syntactic knowledge of language. Therefore from the sound of the predicted word he may try to check whether some or all of those sounds do occur in the print.

Most beginning reading programmes bring children in classrooms to the awareness of sound sequences in words rather effortlessly. For many decades and in many different programmes teachers have taught children to distinguish between letters and to link sounds to those letters. The children who succeeded in those programmes were able to do just that. However, some children find it extraordinarily difficult to hear the sounds that go to make up words. For example, some children consistently focus on the final sound of the word and for them this completely masks the initial sounds.

For children who cannot hear the order of sounds in words the teacher can act as analyser of the words. She articulates the words slowly, but naturally, and gradually develops the same skill in her pupils. It is an essential feature of the theory behind this tutoring to hear the sounds within words that the child's first lessons take place *in the absence of letters or printed words*. The child must *hear* the word spoken, or speak it himself and try to break it into sounds by slowly articulating it. He is asked to show what he can hear with *counters* not *letters*.

Recovery procedures

A child needing help in hearing the sounds in words should begin at the beginning of these recovery procedures and work through the early stages slowly or rapidly according to his needs.

Early learning

Establishing the task   In the first few trials the child will be learning what it is the teacher wants him to do. This applies to slow articulation, to clapping or to pushing counters. Take time to make clear what the task involves. This is the first thing to be learned.

Hearing syllables   Because hearing big chunks of sound is easier than discovering single sounds a good first step is to ask the child to clap the parts he can hear in a few words he knows well. Choose words of one and two syllables at first, and later three or four. Repeat this activity from time to time as opportunities arise in connection with reading or writing stories. The activity will help him with the longer words he tries to write into his stories. (See also discussion of onset and rime page 49.)

Hearing the sounds   Prepare for the activities which help children to hear the sounds within words.

- Make a few picture cards for simple words such as *cat, bus, boy, ship, house* to use to introduce the task.
- Prepare some cards on which you draw a square for each sound segment in words of two, three and four sounds, for example:

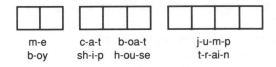

| m-e | c-a-t | b-oa-t | j-u-m-p |
| b-oy | sh-i-p | h-ou-se | t-r-ai-n |

- Have a selection of counters ready.

In the first lessons after the 'roaming around the known' stage only attempt two or three of the activities in the next two lists.

Step I   Slow articulation and hearing sounds

Introduce the child to the task of slowly articulating words. Use a *picture card* and:

- Slowly and deliberately articulate the word for the child. Let him hear the sounds separated but in a natural way.
- Ask the child to articulate the word aloud. Ask him to '*Say it slowly*'. This transfers the initiative for the activity to the child.
- Ask the child to watch your lips while you say it, and then to copy you.
- Use a mirror if it helps the child to be more aware of what his lips and tongue are doing.

Use stress to emphasise any sound you want the child to notice.

Step II   Using the boxes for hearing the sounds in the words you want to write (phonemic analysis)

The sound segment cards make a visual model within which to place the sounds that have been articulated. (Choose a card which has a square for *each sound* in your demonstration word, i.e., a three-square card for c-a-t.) *You need a square for every sound in the aural task, NOT for every letter.* The transfer to an emphasis on letters comes much later.

- Model the task for the child. Articulate the word very slowly and push the counters into the boxes, sound by sound.
- Now get the child to try this. Share the task with the child as long as he finds the coordination of saying slowly and pushing counters too difficult.
  - Articulate the word slowly for him while he moves the counters.
  - Or, get the child to articulate slowly while you push the counters.
  - Change roles to enable the child to practise both parts.
- You may guide the child's hand or work alongside him with another card.
- As soon as possible have the child complete the whole task himself.

Accept his approximations. Coordination will come with practice.

Intermediate steps

Now use words which the child wants to write in his stories and draw boxes on his practice page. Limit the words for this activity to up to four sounds at first. The focus is on hearing sounds and clusters of sounds, and finding some way to record them in letters. This helps the child to write words he has not yet learned to spell.

Select activities like those in the following list according to a particular child's needs.

- Articulate the word slowly for the child, emphasising the sounds.
- Draw a box for each sound segment on the work page of the child's writing book.
- Encourage the child to say the word slowly and push counters into the boxes you have drawn. Later he will not need counters: he will only need to point to each box as he says the word slowly.

- Ask: *'What can you hear?'*
  Accept any sound that the child can hear clearly but cannot write and write it in for him as he watches.
- Ask: *'How would you write it?'*
- Ask: *'Now where will you put it?'*
  Let the child record any sound for which he knows the letter but ensure that it goes in the correct box (i.e. for a time the teacher will need to show the child where to put it). Encourage the child to write all the letters he knows.
- Say: *'How would you write it?'* if the child gives the sound but hesitates over writing the letter(s). If the child cannot recall the letter form give him some help.
  - Make links with what he knows somewhere else — in his alphabet book, or his name, or a word he can already write, or a word in his reading.
  - Provide a magnetic letter or some other model of the letter that the child has forgotten how to write.
  - Let the child who thinks he knows but is unsure do a trial letter on the work page or write the letter in the air or with his finger on the desk.

Then use questions like these to help the child locate other letters.

- What else can you hear?
- What do you hear at the beginning?
- What do you hear at the end?
- What do you hear in the middle?

Accept what the child can hear in any order. Do not insist on a beginning to end approach. This will come later, as the child gains control of the task.

The child can record only those letters he knows how to form and the one or two he is currently learning. The teacher can act as his scribe to produce words like these,

with the child writing only those letters he knows.

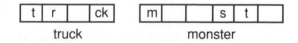

Alternatively, the teacher may get the child to fill in what he can by himself and then complete the word for him, perhaps *teaching one new point* but not explaining everything.

Gradually shift from the question 'What can you hear?' to the question 'What letters would you expect to see?'

A note on consonants and vowels
Be satisfied if the child can separate out some of the consonants. Give the child the vowels as these seem to be much more difficult to hear and require more experience with reading and writing.

For the teacher who is not used to a linguist's analysis of the sounds of spoken English *there are traps* in this activity. For example, one child responding well to her own phonemic analysis of *cousins* wrote:

Kusns

Except for the *Ss* which should have been *Zs* (if you are writing the sounds or phonemes in *cousins*) this is an accurate rendering of the sounds in the word but not one which helped the child to reach the written form of the word. It was not an appropriate word for training sound to letter analysis.

The teacher must be alert to detect the difference between what is good analysis of sounds and what is confusion or error. Here are some examples of accurate 'hearing' by children which should not be undervalued.

| plac | aftr | childrn |
| (place) | (after) | (children) |

There will be an improvement in recording sounds heard as the child identifies more letters and vice versa.

Choosing the words to use in boxes
The teacher must select some of the words which the child wants to write in his stories as the ones most appropriate for learning to hear the sounds in words. How will she choose these? Select on the basis of what will be easiest for this child at this time. At first choose

- words in which it is easy to hear the sounds (not *saw*)
- words which use letters he already knows (not *bed* or *dog*)
- words he will need to use often (not *picture*)
- words which have simple letter-sound relationships in English (this is NOT the place to learn words like *light* or *know* or *police* or *eight*)
- words which will lead him to other words (rather than words which are exceptional in English orthography like *was* or *there*).

Remember to limit the words for this activity to four sounds because more than four sounds can be a problem to the beginner.

Despite all the above at some time during the programme the child will be ready for the teacher to break

with those restrictions. This is a matter of teacher judgement on the basis of her records and knowledge of the particular learner at a particular time in his programme.

Advanced learning
Step 1   Hearing and recording sounds in sequence
If it has not already occurred it is important now to make another special transition as soon as possible. Have the child identify the first sound in the word, and the rest in sequence. This requires him to shift from recording whatever he is able to hear, irrespective of position in the word. Have the child fill in the letters in the boxes *in sequence, from beginning to end, from left to right.*

Step II   Attending to spelling using boxes for letters
After the early learning and intermediate steps the child is usually able to

- hear and record the consonants well
- have control over writing letters
- select some vowels correctly.

If the teacher has noted these kinds of transitions she will decide that he is ready for another important transition.

Now the teacher shifts, and draws a box for every letter in the word to be analysed. She explains this to the child.

At this stage we introduce the child to the mismatch between the sounds of the language to which he has been attending and the way we spell the words. Now we want to provide the child with a box for each letter, even though two letters may not represent two sounds.

One of our teachers found an easy way to introduce the transition:

1) she drew enough boxes for the sounds only and then
2) she put in a dotted line to divide any box that needed two letters like this:

| h | a | m | m | e | r |

and then gradually transferred to solid lines.

Explain the shift to the child — a box for every letter he needs.

- Articulate the word clearly for the child. Let him hear the sounds in sequence several times.
- Make a squared diagram in his booklet with spaces equal to the number of *letters* required.
- Help the child to fill in the letters of the word using stress or pausing on a sound in an exaggerated way to emphasise the sound you want him to focus on.

- As soon as the child can attend to the sound, return to a natural rate and mode of articulation.
- Find similar sound segments in known words.

mother
monster
water
over

- Help the child if the word has unusual elements or ones that he is not yet ready for (especially vowels).

Sometimes our teachers have provided children with some of the letters for vowels and asked them to select the letter they think could be right. It is not clear how helpful this is.

Step III   Working without boxes

In the later stages of a Reading Recovery programme the writing of the word in boxes will not be needed very often.

As the child becomes a better reader and writer he will continue to encounter new words and the following activities will be needed from time to time.

- The child hears the teacher slowly articulating the sounds in sequence, perhaps several times.
- Encourage the child to 'say it slowly'.
- Use stress to emphasise a sound you want him to focus on.
- Use pausing on that sound or draw it out in an exaggerated way to call attention to it.

Return to any of the earlier ways of helping children to hear sounds in words.

A brief overview

The task has been to teach children that a good way to write new words in English is to try to hear the sounds in words, but that this will not always give you the right solution.

- Sometimes you can analyse new words you want to write.
- Sometimes you have to know how to spell a particular word.
- Sometimes you have to 'make it like another word you know' which means get it by analogy with a common spelling pattern used in English.

Remember to direct the child to what he knows in reading to help him with his writing.

7   ASSEMBLING CUT-UP STORIES*

Introduction

Cut-up stories provide the child with practice for:

- assembling sentences
- one-to-one correspondence of words spoken and words written
- directional behaviours
- checking behaviours
- monitoring behaviours
- breaking oral language into segments
- word study (from occasionally cut-up words).

The puzzle-type task on known text can be used for home practice. The written story on the blank page of the child's writing book or on the envelope that holds the cut-up words provides a correct model which he may or may not consult, as needs be.

Recovery procedures

The teacher usually asks the child to reread his story from his unlined book while she writes it again on light cardboard.

Cut up the story into language units which you know the child will be able to reassemble and have him read from the card as you cut it up. Use larger segments for poorer readers. The descending order of size will be

- phrases
- words

and only for particular teaching purposes, structural segments within words to call his attention to

- endings like *ing, s, ed*
- syllables in two-syllable words like *ba/by*
- the rhyming part of a one-syllable word like *s/and* or *w/ent* (called breaking the onset from the rime)
- clusters of letters you think he knows
- single letters at the beginning of words.

---

* Cut-up stories were first demonstrated to me at a conference in Hamilton, New Zealand, by Dr Max Kemp who was using them with older children with reading difficulties for achieving some more advanced concepts of how texts work. Probably the use of this procedure in Reading Recovery does not do justice to his original concept but his contribution to many children's success must be acknowledged.

If you want to cut up a word into syllables or onset and rime segments (see pages 43–47) ask the child to clap the syllables of the word to show you where to cut the word.

Get the child to reassemble the cut-up story, reading as he does so if this helps. This usually calls for careful self-monitoring and checking but it can be made easy or more difficult in the following ways.

- Assembly on top of the model is a matching response – **easy**
- Assembly below the model is a matching response – **harder**
- Assembly without the model is a reading response – **hard**

Then if the assembled cut-up story contains errors, say 'Something's not quite right', calling for a self-monitoring response.

If errors remain then get the child to reread with careful word-by-word matching to the syllable level if this was used.

An example at a very early stage
- The child was asked to tell a story and could not be encouraged to put pencil to paper.
- The teacher offered to write that story in his book. She wrote it again on light cardboard.
- The child pointed to *A* and said he could do that one. (The teacher missed the opportunity to have him write what little he knew.)
- The teacher read the written text and modelled pointing behaviour.
- The child tried inaccurately.
- The teacher guided his hand.
- The child tried accurately.
- The teacher did not cut the story into phrases, which might have been the appropriate teaching step. She emphasised its word components by reading each word as she chopped it off.
- The child reassembled the story matching it on top of the story in his book. It became a *visual matching* exercise rather than a *reading task*. The last word, *bus*, was matched but reorientated 180°.
- The teacher asked him to turn it around and put the tall one on that (left) side. Note that he knew *s* and in *snq* it is correctly orientated.

How children work at a later stage
As the cut-up sentence is assembled the children often verbalise their message. They match what they are saying aloud to what they are doing as they work on searching for each appropriate word, part of a word or particular letter. They keep pace with their voices as they progress with the remaking. At some points children may help their searching or mark time by repeating the word, letter or cluster they are looking for. Sometimes they comment aloud as they search saying, for example 'Where is it? Where is it?' Sometimes they talk about the self-corrections they are making, saying 'No, that's not it.' Final successful completion may be evaluated with a flourishing 'There!' or a grin at their success before rereading for checking. Such verbalised reactions are less likely to occur as children gain increasing competency with reading and writing.

8   READING BOOKS

Introduction

There are twin aims achieved in the book-reading section of Reading Recovery lessons.

- One is to allow the child scope for practising the orchestration of all the complex range of behaviours he must use (and this is best achieved on easy or familiar texts).
- The other is to encourage him to use his reading strategies on novel texts and to support his tentative efforts.

A critical difficulty for some children who seem to have many particular skills and a fair grasp of certain items of knowledge is the using of such assets in the sequential sorting process of reading continuous text. The Reading Recovery procedures provide three opportunities for fostering the bringing together of different kinds of information (the integration of things one knows):

- in reading text (see below)
- in writing and rereading his own stories (see page 28)
- in reconstructing cut-up versions of those stories (see above).

Recovery procedures

Choice of book
Choose the reading book very carefully. First of all take meaning and language into account. Then from the possible texts select one that is well within the child's control, uses words and letters he knows or can get to using his present strategies. There should be a minimum of new things to learn if the teaching goal is the integration of all these aspects of the task.

Orientation to the story before reading*

Introduce the book and make the child familiar with *the story, the plot, the words, the sentences and the writing style*. For example, a teacher might:

- Draw the child's attention to the important ideas.
- Discuss the pictures of the *whole* book.
- Give opportunities for the child to *hear* the new words which he will have to guess from the pictures and language context.
- Ask him to find one or two new and important words in the text after he has said what letter he would expect to see at the beginning.

This effort to facilitate responding might be explained in terms like recency and familiarity. Another explanation is that the teacher is ensuring that the child has in his head the ideas and the language he needs to produce when prompted in sequence by print cues. (See Clay, 1991b.) He should know what the story is about before he reads it.

First reading of the book with help ...

Prepared by such an introduction the child reads the new material as independently as possible. Reading a whole story provides the child with a story structure or framework within which to work out how the story is told. Therefore it is more helpful to select a short story than to ration the exposure to something like 'half the book today' if this is possible. The overall aim is to provide opportunities for the child to

- read as much as possible independently
- engage in 'reading work' to problem-solve difficulties
- get help from a teacher who prompts, confirms and reinforces appropriate behaviours.

In the early part of a child's programme encourage strong, definite locating behaviours, getting the child to point to each word with the index finger to achieve crisp word-by-word integration of point-say-look behaviours.

Support the child with any particular features that are likely to cause him difficulty. For example, provide a model which emphasises by stress, shouting, singing or some other means the anticipated difficulty. In this example *early* was expected to present a particular child with a problem.

> The daisy is asleep
> **early** in the morning.

* Orientation (by the child) means the adjustment or alignment of oneself or one's ideas to surroundings or circumstances.

...or with minimum help

With a child who is using cues appropriately from all areas, and is on the way to independence, say, '*I want you to look at all the pictures and tell me what the story is about. Then I want you to read it all by yourself. I am not going to help unless you really can't do it.*' This shift to providing less support in the book introduction may mean that some other support will be needed again for a period in the first reading. For example, the teacher may need to encourage the child to point during this transition or she may point for him and fail to move on when he makes an error that she thinks he could self-correct.

Teaching during the first reading

The teacher's prompts and other responses during the reading have two aims:

- to shape up and improve the processing of information on continuous texts (the orchestration of efficient reading)
- to direct the child's attention to things he overlooks.

The teacher helps the child to get to information from print to facilitate the reading of the story.

The teacher can do several things which help the child to direct his attention appropriately.

- *Prompt to the error*, i.e., prompt in a helping way that directs the child's attention straight to the information needed to solve the problem. Note that this is like modelling: it tells the child the most advantageous move to make. On the other hand, vague, somewhat related prompting takes the child away from the 'right moves to make'.
- *Give the child some information.* This is not the same as telling the child the word, but like direct prompting to the error it provides the child with a good model of what to attend to next. Prompt for the type of information you want the child to attend to—plot, meaning, language, print, etc.
- Avoid too much questioning at this time because it disrupts the story. Stay close to the problem-solving of this text and the reading of this story as a whole. *Section 9 treats this topic more extensively.*

Having made an excellent choice of books, with challenges matched to the child's learning needs, the teacher should avoid unnecessary interruption of the flow of story reading by making links to other things the child knows, or by making a new teaching point. In the interest of retaining the support of the story and the meaning these teaching points should be left until after the first reading.

Comment positively when the child corrects himself. Reinforce self-correction especially if the child tries to use the kind of cue he has previously avoided. Talk about self-correction. Say how much you like it. Say 'I liked the way you did that.' This is a very useful comment. It approves the process the child was using. It allows the teacher to follow up by directing attention to some new feature, saying, 'But did you notice . . . ?' Such commenting must be done without interrupting the story, but fits comfortably into pauses as the pages are turned.

Teaching after the first reading

During the first reading of a new text there may be some things that the teacher wants to talk over with the child — perhaps the child did some remarkable solving, or perhaps he got close to the meaning of the text but overlooked some useful information. So after the reading the teacher could turn back to the page involved and say things like

- I liked the way you solved the puzzle on this page. Do you remember where you had to work it out? How did you do that? (See page 47 on verbalising the process.)
- Look at this word. You said 'home'. Is it 'home'? What can you see near the end?
- Let's take a look at what the rabbit said on this page. You said 'I think we shall (should) go and find him.' Is that what the rabbit said? Read it again, and see if you can find the tricky word.

The teacher would be making careful decisions about what to attend to, *selecting only one or two points*. If the book has been carefully chosen to suit the child's current competencies there should be only a few things to discuss. The kinds of things that teachers attend to would change over time as readers become more competent.

This is a good place to make more links to other knowledge the child has.

Rereading for fluency

If the first reading was not very successful and was interrupted by a large amount of processing or reading work, have the child reread the story for a second time in the *same lesson* to get a flow of words and a real feel for the story. The teacher may want to read with the child, staying one step behind the child on problem words to check on how he manages these. Such rereading would occur rarely in the later stages of a child's programme.

Home and school practice

Accumulate a box of familiar books and reread a selection of these each session, say two or three at the beginning of the lesson. *A familiar book is not a memorised book!* It is a book which still challenges the child to do some reading work, engaging with print, and picking up new information. Although a child reads a book with a high level of accuracy there may be many features of the text which have not yet come to his notice. The practice of rereading familiar books encourages confidence and fluency, and provides practice in bringing reading behaviours together (orchestration) but it also allows the reader to discover new things about print during the rereading. The control over the text allows attention to shift to features of the text or the story not previously attended to.

Get the child to read easy books at home for independent practice.

A child who is on the way to independence needs as many books as possible at his level. Allow the child to learn to read by reading many books.

A second reading of the book next day

When a book has been introduced and read once be ready to take a Running Record at the next session. After the reading check the record for any processing problems (not making sense, not noticing errors, not monitoring carefully, not cross-checking or using visual cues); and any remaining errors such as:

- use of structural features, *s, ed, ing*
- matching with finger
- segmenting the sentence or word
- asking 'What letters do you expect to see?'

Here is an example of a check on an easy book.

- The teacher reads the title, *Who are you?* and asks the child to read it with his finger. The teacher can observe directional behaviour and speech-to-print matching.
- The child is invited to organise and control his own reading behaviour independently.
- The child reads the book and the teacher takes a Running Record.
- The child read *bears* for *elephants* and corrects himself. So, when he has finished his teacher says, 'What does elephants start with?' an invitation for aural analysis of *e* in *elephants* and a sound-to-letter association.
- The teacher quickly checks some knowledge of individual words which were teaching points for this book. She uses a sliding mask card to efficiently and swiftly isolate the word, and asks 'What is that?' The child responds with speed. She includes a question about punctuation.

After this second reading this book is placed in the child's box of familiar books, the ones he has read previously. The teacher will from time to time remove the books which no longer challenge the child because he knows them so very well. She will also remove a book if she thinks the child has memorised it because the child no longer has any reason to search the print for information to guide his reading. The memorised book will not challenge him to carry out 'reading work'.

9 TEACHING FOR STRATEGIES

Introduction

Many theories of reading are theories of reading words in isolation but little children engage with books at the level of the story, not with isolated words. Children like to read stories and they learn a great deal about print and texts as they do this. The comments in this section apply mostly to reading continuous texts.

On new or novel texts children must engage in 'reading work'. This is where they increase their power over the reading task. They solve their problems by using their theories of the world and their theories of written language. They cross-check in their heads which options are most likely. This reading work can be *heard* in the early stages of reading progress but it becomes a silent process. These monitoring and problem-solving strategies or operations going on in the child's head are more powerful than some of the weaker, overt procedures that teachers have encouraged children to use, like sounding out the word or reading on.

Good readers

Reading instruction often focuses on items of knowledge — words, letters, sounds. Most children respond to this teaching in active ways. They search for links between the items and they relate new discoveries to old knowledge. They operate on print as Piaget's children operate on problems, searching for relationships which order the complexity of print and therefore simplify it. For such children the teaching sequence described in these teaching procedures is unnecessary.

Poor readers

Children who fail to progress in reading do not approach print in this way. The operations which they have tried to carry out have not brought order to the complexity and they have often become passive in their confusion.

This section offers suggestions which have proved useful in getting passive poor readers to become more active in searching for cues, predicting possible responses and verifying these responses.

A self-extending system

The end-point of such instruction is reached when children have a self-extending system — a set of operations just adequate for reading a slightly more difficult text for the precise words and meanings of the author.

When we operate or work on a problem we are engaged in a conscious search for solutions. In reading we sometimes consciously search for a word or a meaning or a correction but most of the time our active search is a fast reaction of the brain that seems to be automatic and not conscious. Perhaps strategies is a better name for these fast reactions used while reading.

Recovery procedures: operations or strategies used on texts

A child can only acquire and practise these important operations or strategies on texts as he reads books and rereads the stories he has written. Children begin to discover what strategies they can use on text for themselves on their very first encounters with books.

It has been erroneously reported that in Reading Recovery children are expected to memorise the texts of their first books in order to match what they have learned by heart with what they see on the page (Ehri and Sweet, 1991). Such a memorising strategy would be antagonistic to what the reader has to do: the on-going problem-solving of the reader on continuous text has nothing in common with memorising the text first. Memorising is NOT a place to begin because it gives the novice reader an incorrect impression of what the task is.

At an early stage of his programme the child begins by bringing his knowledge of language, and his knowledge of the world, and his knowledge of the ways in which books work to bear on the pictures and text of a particular, and not at all difficult, text. He may invent a possible text for the first page. The teacher may then model the sentence on that page. She may know that most, but not all, of the sentences in the subsequent pages use the same sentence pattern with only one or two words being varied. Most children work out what the rest of the text may say, trying to match the text to their predictions of what it might say. But from this simple beginning the child is aware that there are ways of working out what the text says in this book and it is the reader's job to find cues which guide him to the meaning.

The child who is getting classroom exposure to story-books, and book sharing, or has had rich preschool experiences with books, will already have this active searching of text behaviour; others will need to build up an awareness of how texts work. Such awareness commonly emerges from hearing stories read and discussed in the classroom and at home.

As to the specific strategies needed to read texts the earliest ones (**1–4**) are very important because through them the child comes to control his visual attention to print. These earliest strategies give the child a means of checking that he is attending to the right part of the page. They are:

1   Directional movement
Ideas for encouraging appropriate directional behaviours have been described already under Learning About Direction (page 19).

2   One-to-one matching
This was discussed in detail under Locating Responses (page 21). Here are some ways to encourage this as the child reads books.

- Say '*Read it with your finger.*'
- Or '*Did that match?*'
- Or '*Were there enough words?*'
- Or '*Did you run out of words?*'
- Accompany the child's pointing with your own pointer and fail to move on when he makes an error that you feel he could self-correct.
- When you want to slow down a too-fluent language response, use two small pieces of card or two fingers to frame each word.

3   Locating one or two known words
On the earliest reading books begin to encourage the child's attention to particular words in continuous text by focusing on words which he knows in any context — home, community, classroom or Reading Recovery.

- *Prompt the child to use a special cue he knows*
  This may be any type of cue. The aim is to have the child take some initiative and do some 'reading work'. You should welcome any contribution the child can make to solving the problem.
- *Tell the child the word*
  Follow this modelling with questions like these (where the word is 'help'):
  '*Would that make sense*?'
  '*Would "help" fit there*?'
  '*Do you think it looks like "help"*?'

After the child has read the whole story with miscues on one or two words which you are sure he knows, turn back and encourage him to locate those items he knows in the text.

- Read back an error sentence to him and ask '*You said . . . Was that right?*'
- Reread the page or sentence up to the known-word-read-wrongly with fluent phrasing and stop, or, if you need to give more help, articulate the first sound of the problem word.

4   Locating an unknown word
As in (**3**) above, but now draw the child's attention to words that are new to him.

Be careful not to establish a pattern where the child waits for the teacher to do the work. This is the point at which the child must learn that he must work at a difficulty, take some initiative, make some links. It is the general principle that needs to be established at this time and *it does not matter which types of cues the child uses.* Different children will use different types, depending upon what is easy for them at this time.

Checking on oneself or self-monitoring

The successful reader who is making no errors is monitoring his reading at all times. Effective monitoring is a highly skilled process constructed over many years of reading. It begins early but must be continually adapted to encompass new challenges in texts.

- To encourage self-monitoring in the very early stages ask the child to go back to one-to-one pointing:
  Say '*Point to each one.*'
  Or '*Use a pointer and make them match.*'
- Direct the child's attention to meaning:
  Say '*Look at the picture.*'
  Or '*Remember that they went to the shop and . . .*'
- For particular attention to an error allow the child to continue to the end of the sentence:
  Say '*I liked the way you did that.*
     Where was the hard bit?'
- If the child gives signs of uncertainty — hesitation, frowning, a little shake of the head — even though he takes no action:
  Say '*Was that OK?*'
  Or '*Why did you stop?*'
  Or '*What did you notice?*'

These questions tell the child that you want him to monitor his own reading. The operation to be learned is checking on oneself. It is more important that the child comes to check on his own behaviour than that he be required to use all the sources of cues at this stage.

- Don't forget to reinforce the child for his self-monitoring attempts whether they are successful or not. Say '*I liked the way you tried to work that out.*'
- Encourage recognition of cues from letter sequences. Let the child predict the word he expects it to be. Cover the problem word and ask for something you know he knows about that word. One of these questions might be useful:
  '*What do you expect to see at the beginning?*'
  '*... at the end?*'
  '*... after the "M"?*'
  Then ask him to check as you uncover the word.
- Ask the child 'Were you right?' after both *correct* and *incorrect* words.
- Ask 'How did you know?' after correct words.
- As the child becomes more skilled do less teaching and prompting and modelling. Merely say 'Try that again' but make sure that your voice carries two messages. You are requiring him to search, because you know he can, and you are confident he can solve the problem.

Remember, though, to give help when it is required.

Cross-checking on information

Cross-checking is a tentative behaviour. It is not possible to be specific about it. One has a hunch that it is happening after observing the child. We must ask 'Is this child checking one kind of information against another?'

Cross-checking is most obvious when a child is not satisfied with a response for some reason. The child may make another attempt, or look back, or think again, or complain that a necessary letter is missing. The child uses two sources of information, checking one against the other. He uses meaning but complains that some letters are not there. He uses visual cues from letters but says that it doesn't make sense.

Some examples of this kind of behaviour are these:

- He can get movement and language occurring together in a coordinated way, and knows when he has run out of words.
- He checks language prediction by looking at some letters.
- He can hear the sounds in a word he speaks and checks whether the expected letters are there.
- After a wrong response he can make another attempt at the word (searching).

- After a wrong response he repeats the sentence, phrase or word, indicating he is aware and trying to get some additional information (repeating).
- After a wrong response he makes a verbal comment about it, e.g., 'No! That's not right!' (commenting on the mismatch).

The teacher must observe what kinds of information the child is using. When the child can monitor his own reading and can search for and use structure or message or sound cues or visual cues, begin to encourage him to check one kind of cue against another. The teacher can

- point up discrepancies — 'It could be ... but look at ...'
- insert possible words so that the child can confirm the response using some letter knowledge
- say 'Check it! Does it look right and sound right to you?'

Cross-checking describes early behaviours. The child learns that one kind of information can be compared with another kind, and all information should agree in the solution. This behaviour is superseded in time by more successful self-correction using many sources of information and 'better quality' substitutions.

A teacher encourages cross-checking behaviour
Teacher: 'What was the new word you read?'
Child: '*Bicycle.*'
           'How did you know it was bicycle?'
           '*It was a bike.*' (semantics)
           'What did you expect to see?'
           '*A "b"?*' (phonology)
           'What else?'
           '*A little word, but it wasn't.*' (size)
           'So, what did you do?'
           '*I thought of bicycle.*' (back to semantics)
           (Reinforcing the checking) 'Good, I liked
           the way you worked at that all by yourself.'

Outcome The child will attend to cross-checking because the teacher attended to it.

Searching for cues

To develop the child's abilities to search for all types of cues use the following set of questions in flexible ways. In your first attempts to call new features of print to the child's attention use the child's present behaviour in your first examples.

- Cues in sentence structure (syntax):
  Say '*You said ... Can we say it that way?*'

- Cues from the message (semantics):
  Say *'You said . . . Does that make sense?'*
- Cues from the letters (graphic cues):
  Say *'Does it look right?'*
- Or more generally:
  Say *'What's wrong with this?'* (repeating what the child said).

As children gain greater control and encounter new words the teacher may say:

- *'Try that again and think what would make sense.'*
- *'Try that again and think what would sound right.'*

If the child has a bias towards letter detail the teacher's prompts will be directed towards the message and the language structure.

- She may need to orient the child to the picture as a meaning source.
- She may need to introduce new vocabulary, as when the problem word was *broth* and the teacher said, *'There was an old lady who lived in a shoe. . .'* and the child said, *'I know—soup!'*
- Sometimes it is necessary for a child to gain control over a particular language structure first, so that he can bring it back to the reading situation.

Four types of cue (technically called information)

From the theory of reading behind these recovery procedures there are many sources of information in texts but during this programme the teachers will pay particular attention to four kinds of information which young readers must learn to look for. Different kinds of information may be checked one against another to confirm a response.

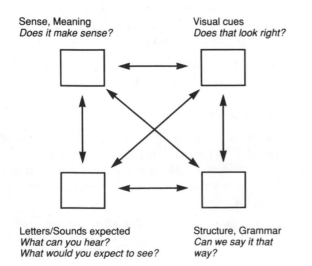

Sense, Meaning
Does it make sense?

Visual cues
Does that look right?

Letters/Sounds expected
What can you hear?
What would you expect to see?

Structure, Grammar
Can we say it that way?

This square is a grossly simplistic diagram and *is not a model of what amazing links the brain is making.* The diagram is drawn to help the teacher think around the 'unseen' behaviours engaged in by the reader.

An example of fostering searching behaviour

Teacher: 'You almost got that page right. There was something wrong with this line. See if you can find what was wrong.'

Child: (Silently rereads, checking) *'I said Lizard but it's Lizard's.'*
'How did you know?'
'Cause it's got an "s".'
'Is there any other way we could know?' (Search further)
(Child reruns in whisper) *'It's funny to say "Lizard dinner"! It has to be Lizard's dinner like Peter's dinner, doesn't it?'*
(Reinforcing the searching) 'Yes. That was good. You found two ways to check on that tricky new word.'

Outcome   The achievement is not that the child was 'corrected' and got the rendering 'right', but rather that the child will attend to searching because the teacher attended to it.

Self-correction

Very early, on their first books, children begin to correct themselves without any prompting. The child who monitors his own reading, and searches for help (cues) in the text, and cross-checks at least two types of information, will be self-correcting some of his own errors.

- Comment positively on some self-corrections. Say *'I liked the way you found out what was wrong all by yourself.'*
- Allow time for self-correction. The child must take the initiative.
- To make a more confident reader even more independent of the teacher don't do anything when he makes a mistake or stops. Don't give him any clues. Say *'You made a mistake on that page'* (or *'in that sentence'*). *Can you find it?'* This places the responsibility on the child.

A note on verbalising the process

Check on some words accurately read with *'How did you know?'* or *'Were you right?'*

In familiar tasks a young child often comes to a stage where he can comment on what he can do. The question

'*How did you know it was X?*' invites the child to examine his own behaviour after he has successfully carried out some operation in his reading. The teacher may be asking for the child's help so that she can understand this particular strength he has. Occasionally, she may be asking the child to verbalise this to raise his own awareness (although this should not be a common practice, see below).

What is the relationship between the need for fast, automatic responses to words and phrases, and this instructional device which slows up the process and asks the child to think about it? It seems legitimate to encourage a child to verbalise a strategy or a principle or a rule-like consistency because these have more general application. They have generative value. It also seems legitimate to bring to a child's notice a success he has had in mastering a previous difficulty, because confidence has generative value also.

It is a tactic that could be overworked and could interfere with the automatic responding that goes with fluency.

The goal is a self-extending system

Teachers aim to produce independent readers whose reading and writing improve whenever they read and write. In the independent student:

- Early strategies are secure and habituated, freeing the reader to attend to other things.

The child:

- *monitors* his own reading and writing
- *searches* for cues in word sequences, in meaning, in letter sequences
- *discovers* new things for himself
- *cross-checks* one source of cues with another
- *repeats* as if to *confirm* his reading or writing so far
- *self-corrects* taking the initiative for making cues match, or getting words right
- *solves* new words by these means.

Extending these operations

As the child reaches out to more complex texts and writes longer and more involved stories these operations will be used with increasing speed and fluency on:

- longer stretches of meaning
- less familiar language
- less predictable texts.

10   LINKING SOUND SEQUENCE WITH LETTER SEQUENCE

Introduction

How words are constructed

Although it may not be immediately obvious a little thought will confirm that all the words in an English dictionary can be constructed by varying the number and order of 26 letters. Some children who are still preschoolers discover and begin to manipulate this idea: that the letters you know can be used to construct different words.

Taking that discovery further involves several important concepts – the order of letters matters, the first letter is determined by position and not how it looks, and letters link in some vague way to the sounds we speak.

Slowly, throughout the reading and writing work of the Reading Recovery lessons the child is introduced to different ways of

- constructing a new word in writing
- or working out a new word in reading.

(See also Sections 4, 9, and 11.)

Much of the puzzle for the child seems to lie in the hierarchical relationship of letters to words. There is not an easy answer to questions like '*Is this string of letters a word, and if so, what is it?*' What makes a word? As many strings of letters are not words how is a word different from a non-word?

Children seem to make sense of this puzzle as they begin to acquire a writing vocabulary, the words a child knows how to write. Children see similarities in words, similar letters and similar letter sequences. 'The ways words work' become more obvious as the child constructs words in writing (Sections 5 and 6) or engages in making and breaking work, substituting and switching parts of words to other words (see later in this section).

One suspects that the child is building up experience to answer the basic question '*When is a string of letters a word and when is it not?*' A word in English is constructed according to the letter sequences found in English. Time, exposure, construction of words in writing and putting this to work in reading seems to bring the child to a knowledge of how words are made in English.

The accumulation of reading and writing vocabulary contributes to this awareness of the ways words are made. Two other conditions in the learner must be fostered by the teacher. Firstly, the child must learn to work actively on constructing words in writing or analysing words while reading. Secondly, the teacher must demonstrate and make clear that what the child knows in writing can be of use to him in reading and vice versa. I refer to this as the reciprocity of the two activities that both use written language. The relatedness of these two areas may not be evident to the learner who needs encouragement to use what he knows in writing to help him read in reading, and vice versa.

Sound sequences and letter sequences

It is useful to remember that whenever a child reads a piece of text aloud he is achieving a coordination of sound sequence with letter sequence. Thousands and thousands of these coordinations occur as children read correctly from books.

The skilled reader achieves an exact coordination between what his eye is attending to and what he is saying. (More precisely that should read what his eye has just been attending to and what he is now saying, because his eyes will have moved on to pick up the next set of visual cues.)

At times there are words to be read which are new to the child reader and there are many sources of information in text which may enable the reader to 'read' the new word for the first time. However, sometimes the child will need to do some 'reading work' at the word level to discover what the new word is.

In earlier sections ideas were introduced for helping Reading Recovery children to make:

a) an analysis of sounds in spoken words (auditory) (page 32) and

b) an analysis of signs in written words (visual) (page 23).

Reading Recovery teachers find children who can do a) but not b) and vice versa. They also find children who can do both a) and b) as separate activities but cannot link one with the other.

The activities listed in this section were found useful in developing links between *how the child analyses the sounds of words he needs to write or words he anticipates in his reading texts,* and *how the child analyses the letters and letter clusters in a word in his reading against the word he is trying to say.*

This is not a simple problem of phonics. This is a difficult task of coordinating two complex sets of operations—sound sequence analysis and letter sequence analysis. It is also partly based on tacit knowledge that letters are likely to occur in certain sequences in English and that knowledge is only acquired by reading quantities of print.

In Reading Recovery we find children who need extra help to begin to make these links for themselves, but once they understand the nature of the task they begin to teach themselves in ways that are more efficient than any sequenced instruction programme could hope to be.

If the child can move easily from sounds to letters or from letters to sounds he is easily prompted by the teacher, who can say, '*Check to see if what you read looks right and sounds right to you.*' Some children are unable to initiate such checks.

Recovery procedures

When the child knows at least twenty letters

When the child has some letter identification knowledge to work with spend only part of the letter identification time in the lesson on letters, and do some work with *words in isolation.* At first use only known words, for what has been called 'making and breaking' among Reading Recovery teachers in New Zealand.* We are talking about one or two minutes initially and no more than three minutes in later lessons.

During writing the child will be constructing words as he composes his text; in reading books the child will be taking some words apart to discover what they are. In making and breaking the child will be doing both these activities *in order to become more aware of how to work with what he knows, to get to new words.* Its intent is to help the child to understand the process of word construction, how words work, and how he can get help from words he knows to use on new words he needs to know.

Making and breaking with magnetic letters

The action of making and breaking

First we have to help the child to understand the task. Give the child the correct magnetic letters and ask him to make a word he knows on the magnetic board. (Words as simple as *is/his* and *he/me* would do.) Make him construct the word and break it apart several times.

Say '*Look at the word. Say it slowly and run your finger under it.*'

Work with many familiar words so he begins to understand how letters make up words, and how words can be taken apart, letter by letter, or in clusters (for example, adding inflections like *ing, s, ed,* and taking them away).

---

* Clay, 1979, pp. 60–63, 77; Bradley, 1980; Iversen, 1991, modified for experimental treatment; Clay, this edition. Revisions relate to recent research on phonological awareness, onset and rime, and analogy.

What makes it easy?

Several things can make making and breaking easy, as it should be until the child understands how to work this way.

- Using the hand and eye on the manipulation task (this is important).
- Having all the letters or words supplied for the child by the teacher.
- Breaking at 'easy-to-find' breaks within the word such as inflections, syllables, and onset and rime breaks.

We all know that little children like to play with rhymes. Recent research has shown that many children who enter school have a useful awareness of two parts in a single-syllable word — a beginning part and a rhyming part. The beginning part is being called by linguists the onset (which is made up of consonants at the beginning of the word) and the second part is called the rime (or the rhyming part of the word).

Whenever word work is being done (in reading, in writing, or at the magnetic board) the teacher should remember that children can hear syllables, and rimes. From rimes they can discover onsets.

As children appear to work not only with letters and sounds but also with *clusters of letters* and *chunks of sound* making new words by analogy with old words, we could probably make learning easier if we avoided instruction which conflicts in any way with this prior learning about language that children have. This means that in making and breaking at the magnetic board, and while helping children in their writing, the teacher should observe what clusters a particular child can use, clusters larger than letter-sound associations.

Simple analogies

Take a set of very easy and very familiar words like *go, so, no*. Construct two of them slowly, ask the child to construct the third and then to read all the words.

A harder task is to take a word like *he*, give the child an *m*, and ask him to change the *he* to *me*. The *he, me, we* set is an easy one to work with.

Using predictable (regular) letter-sound sequences

Give the child experience on words he knows but which you have chosen very carefully because the sounds match with the spelling (like *went/sent*, and *look/book*, but not *box/socks*). Although the child knows the words the teacher could provide the first word and all the letters needed to go from *hat/mat*, or *like/bike*.

Pairs of words like *went/sent* change the onset but retain the rime. Pairs of words like *bell/ball* change the end part but retain the onset.

It suits the purposes of the novice reader to derive a new word from the sound of one he knows, asking himself, '*Do I know a word that sounds like this one?*'

- If he chooses a suitable analogy and solves the new word the teacher can praise him for how he solved the problem.
- If he makes a wrong assumption about a word, for example he pronounces *wash* and *mash* as a rhyming pair the teacher can say '*Well, it might have worked like that but this word says...*' giving him the correct sound sequence for the letter sequence.

Now have the child think of the words

As the child's control of this task is increasing the teacher asks the child to bring more to the activity. The initial word might be the child's choice, or he may be asked to make a rhyming word, and sometimes he might give two or three words which sound like each other. The important shift is that the child will be applying the process of making and breaking to words he thinks of by himself — he will provide the examples.

There is a risk in this activity. Before long the child may begin to think that probably all words will fit into spelling sequences which can be pronounced in one way. This, of course, is not how English words work so he must make some more discoveries.

Using less predictable letter-sound sequences

The emphasis shifts to include rimes which may not be clearly soundable because there are competing ways of pronouncing them. The spelling pattern may have alternative pronunciations, and/or all the letters may not be sounded. Consider, for example,

hear	*near*	*bear*
come	*some*	*home*

To increase the difficulty of the task as the child's competence increases move through a sequence something like this —

supply the letters and/or models
substitute onsets
then rimes
the child thinks of other known words
the child makes up other words that are new to him.

In many classrooms around the world while teachers

have been teaching 'phonics' children have probably been learning something much more useful. They have been constructing the complex associations between sound sequences and letter sequences that enable us to become fluent readers of three categories of words in English:

1 those with sound sequences which can be predicted from the letters (*jump, left, went)*

2 those with alternate letter-sound correspondences, because there may be two or more ways of saying the same spelling pattern (for example, the child might say *'Is it "ow" in owl, or "ow" in slow?')*

3 those that are better described as orthographic or spelling sequences than sound sequences (*the, then, they*). There are also more tricky words in this category which Reading Recovery children might not need to read while they are on the programme, words in which the letter sequences are misleading if one tries to relate them to sounds (*know, write, break, cough*).

Continue to explore how words work

There is no end to the permutations of making and breaking as the child becomes more proficient as a reader and writer and his word knowledge increases. Teachers must beware that learning how words work does not degenerate into *teaching words* for that is not the purpose of this part of the lesson. There are many intricacies of the English language that can be explored and discussed with the child. Things that are new to him can be

- contrasted with what he already knows
- or paired with a like word
- or set out on their own as quite new.

When the child gains control over working with pronounceable onsets and rimes, and spelling patterns which are not pronounced as they are spelled, he discovers some of the tricks of some English words which occur quite early in reading books like *home/come* and *go/to*. Children do not need a verbal explanation of the differences. Rather they need to be ready for the fact that 'this one is different.' It is as if many words fit with some kind of rule but these are the different ones, the exceptions.

Think about what you say

Some of the things that teachers teach are not consistent with the way English sounds. When teachers teach about making words plural they teach children to add an *s*, but if you listen to the word *cousins* you will hear two *z* sounds. When teachers teach about the past tense of the verb they

will tell the child to add *ed*, and pronounce it *d*. But if you listen carefully to yourself pronouncing these three words

stopped   *slammed*   *wanted*

you might hear three different sounds or sound clusters. One spelling pattern does for three quite different pronunciations!

So be careful when you tell children about the ways in which words are the same and different. Think about the sounds, and the spellings, and make sure teacher and child both know which parts are 'the same' and in what way!

If the child finds it hard to go from sounds to letters

This may hold up his progress with making and breaking. In his reading a child may focus on letters and be able to remember the sounds they make and yet that child may find it difficult to go from hearing the sounds in words to producing the letters he needs to represent those sounds in making and breaking.

Get the child to articulate the word he wants to make slowly (pushing counters into boxes if necessary for each sound he can hear). This was described earlier (see page 32). Pay attention to this in writing.

If the child finds it hard to go from letters to sounds

A child may be able to analyse sounds to letters in his writing and with the help of word boxes but may not be able to use letter-to-sound associations to help him eliminate miscues in his reading. Pay attention to this in reading.

Using his own written stories

- Get the child to remake his own stories that have been rewritten on paper strips and cut up (Section 7, page 35). The sounds of the story are in his head and he uses these as a guide to finding the words he has written.
- Ask the child to clap syllables and show him where to cut a word into two parts. Then get him to remake the story.

On his reading books

- When the child comes to a problem word in the text, sound the initial letter for him to help him to predict what the right word might be. Then transfer this sounding task to him by getting him to attend to the initial letter or letters and to get his mouth ready to say it. The aim is to make him more conscious of a strategy that will help him to eliminate the words that would fit the context but not the first letter cues.

- If he has good mastery of sound-to-letter analysis but yet does not independently attempt some analysis of simple words in text, write them letter by letter on the blackboard, getting him to articulate the accumulating letters until the word that would fit the context comes into his head

c   cr-   cr-ash.

Making this operation more explicit

Check on some words accurately read with '*How did you know?*' or '*Were you right?*'

In reading instruction, this invites the child to examine his own behaviour after he has successfully applied the necessary operations to his reading. For example:

> The child read *from* as *for* in a sentence and corrected himself.
> The teacher asked '*Is it from?*'
> The child replied '*It starts with f.*'
> The teacher said '*So does for.*'
> The child said '*It ends with m.*'

It seems legitimate to encourage a child to verbalise these operations from time to time as a check on what he is doing. Verbalising is a tactic that could be overworked however, and could interfere with the fast responding that is required for fluency. (See also page 38.)

Do not get carried away

The child should learn about constructing words and taking words apart in many places in his lessons. The aim of this work is to have him know about how words work and be able to use this awareness on reading texts in reading and while writing. To be able to work on words in isolation is not enough; the reader and writer must also work on words in continuous texts.

11 TAKING WORDS APART IN READING

Introduction

If the child is writing stories and doing an efficient sound-to-letter analysis of the new words he wants to write, the problem to be faced by the teaching procedures in this section is *what sort of analysis of new words can the teacher help the child to do in his reading?*

Most schemes for teaching word analysis begin with the assumptions that:

- the teacher needs an instructional sequence
- this can be arrived at by some logical ordering process.

In these Reading Recovery procedures we have assumed that the goal of tutoring is to achieve the most rapid acceleration possible for the child, and, therefore:

- that the child's skills should determine the sequence
- that the word segments attended to should be those used by good readers at this level of learning to read
- that the sequence should be ordered by psychological rather than logical factors.

Following these assumptions and referring to research on early reading it has been found

- *that final letters* or *initial letters* are the starting points for a child's detailed analysis of words
- that *inflections* added to words are easy to recognise
- that an early achievement is to know that you work left to right across a word
- that consonants in the word are quite easy to deal with
- that easy-to-hear vowels are somewhat more difficult
- and that there are very hard-to-hear consonants or vowels.

This is not a teaching sequence, nor should it guide the teacher's expectations. Any individual child may deviate from that description. On the average something like that occurs.

Now, good readers read in chunks. They attach sounds to a group of letters (rather than each letter) if that works. So if the child attends to a large chunk or group of letters within words be careful not to make him think that this is wrong! He can learn letter-by-letter analysis, left to right, on other words and particularly in his writing.

The aim is to have the child use what he knows, and this is in conflict with many reading programmes which insist on directing the child's attention to the smallest units first. Let's start with an example of a competent child in his first year at school, picking his own way through the analysis of words, just because it's interesting!

John's progress was exceptional. When he entered school he was part of a research study and was given, among other assessments, a readiness test. He scored below the norms on the test, almost as low as a child could get, and he came from a home that was not particularly interested in schooling. It is only possible to guess why his progress was so good, even though I had weekly records of his literacy learning. It was certainly facilitated by the fact that nine months after entry to school John became a commentator on the code. He was interested in words and their possibilities and was actively verbalising his comparisons of what he saw with what he remembered, noting features that did and did not fit with certain ways of categorising words. For example he would say:

'Look!
If you cover up *painting* you get *paint*.
If you cover up *shed* you get *she*.
If you cover *o* in *No* you don't get anything.
I've is like *drive* but it's *have*.
That looks like *Will* but it's *William*.'

John was very advanced in his approach to taking words apart. He could use inflections, he could use alternative sound renderings, he understood contractions, and proper name conventions. He was a successful reader and a successful analyser of words. He was aware of much more than letter-sound relationships!

The teacher must be a careful observer. The child may be attending to only one letter, or only one feature of a letter like the cross on the '*t*' and you may think he is paying attention to the whole word, or clusters of letters. Only a few children like John are able to make it quite clear what they are attending to.

Words may be taken apart and linked to other word knowledge in any part of the lesson, but there is a particular focus on such an activity:

- when making and breaking words in the letter identification section of the lesson
- after familiar book reading
- during the work on the new book
- after the new book.

Recovery procedures

Take words apart only when necessary
Reread Section 4 (page 23) where there is a discussion of the origin of words a teacher could select for attention. It stresses how word work should be integral to the reading and writing of continuous texts.

Initial letters or signs
The following suggestions might be used at any time in the lesson, throughout the series of lessons. Teach a relevant distinction whenever it is important for a particular child to make that distinction (and not as a matter of routine).

In the early lessons supplying magnetic letters during text reading may provide memorable experiences and will demand the least prior knowledge from the child.

Draw attention to initial letters.

- Words that begin with the same sound: *Frank, father: Harry, here.*
- Go from first letter to sound (when looking at print).
- Go from sound to expected first letter (when anticipating how the language of text will go).
- Go from first letter sound to predict the word and say '*What else could you check?*'
- Deal with capital/lower case pairs: *Going, going: Is, is: And, and: Here, here.*

Draw attention to going beyond the initial letter to distinguish confusing words: *and, am: this, the: Andrew, Ann.*

Be alert when the child is reading, and when he is problem-solving call his attention to things he has worked on in writing or while working with magnetic letters.

Final letters or signs
Draw attention to final letters. (Use colour if it helps.)

- The presence of '*s*' as in: plurals, *trees*; possessives, *Lizard's*; verbs, *jumps*.
- The absence of '*s*'.
- Final letters in words like: *it, in, his, him, but, bun, bus, buzz.*
- Attend to punctuation occasionally, like full stops, question, exclamation and speech marks.

Think about what is happening in writing
The child has to discover the significant features in a word that will allow him to distinguish it in reading from other possible words in his experience. The work he does while writing his story for the day can help him to discover significant features which he might meet again in his reading.

In writing, when a child can write a word letter by letter, slowly but correctly, give him more opportunities to do it again, do it quickly, and do it in another place. Such activities call for close attention to the details of words, to making the whole word quickly, and for using those skills in different contexts.

Prepare for using letter groups or chunks of information: Hearing the breaks
As opportunities arise with multisyllabic words ask the child to clap the syllables in two- and three-syllable words.

jum / bo / jet	*par / ty*
el /e / phant	*mo / ther*
Pe / ter	*go / ing*

Helpful questions to prompt solving

The visual analysis of words in text can be encouraged by the teacher's questions as the child reads text.

- After success in word solving.
  Say '*How did you know it was . . .?*'
- When the child stops at a new word.
  Say '*What could you try . . .?*'
  Or '*Do you know a word like that?*'
  Or '*What would you think it could be?*'
  Or '*Do you know a word that starts with those letters?*'
  Or '*What do you know that might help?*'

The teacher is prompting the reader to pay attention to certain features or to the usefulness of analogy (see page 50).

Finding help within the word

What parts of words do children find it easy to work with? We usually think of letters as being the bits out of which words are built but in speech there are several kinds of natural breaks in words. Perhaps the child, who already speaks the language, can get help from these natural breaks in spoken language. These include

- a syllable break
- an inflection break
- prefix or suffix breaks

and recent publications introduce us to

- the onset and rime break.

This is the break between initial consonant or consonant cluster and the rest of the word. Here are some examples:

> *tr-ain   s-ent   sp-ent   spr-ing*

One way to think of the final cluster in these words is that it makes up the rhyme in poetry and nursery jingles and songs, but the linguist's term is 'rime'. Research shows that it is quite easy for speakers to break the single-syllable word at the onset and rime break. So we should keep all these types of breaks in mind as we prompt children to take words apart in some useful ways.

An example of fostering the use of letter clusters

The child, reading the word *joking*, stops.
Teacher: (prompting) 'What does it start with?'
Child: '*j*'
Teacher: 'Can you say more than that?'
Child: '*jo--k . . . joke*'

Teacher: 'Is the end of joke right?'
Child: '*ing . . . joking*'
Teacher: 'Yes. You found two parts to that word, *jok* and *ing*. We could look at other words like that, *taking, jumping*. Let's go on with the story.'

Help in taking words apart while reading

The goal of all forms of word analysis for the reader is to be able to take words apart, on the run, while reading—unexpected known words, partially familiar words still being learned and new, unknown words. This section focuses on some things to do that will help the reader do this without slowing down the reading too much.

When you want the reader to think about adding, or subtracting, or substituting letters when he is problem-solving in reading you may need to point to or write the word he is focusing on, quickly, on a whiteboard or on paper.

It is always easier if the teacher supplies all the material (letters, written words) that are needed for the solving.

Taking words apart after reading books

A little more word work on taking words apart may follow the reading of a book.

Adding   Being asked to add to words that you know seems to be one of the easy tasks. Adding any one of the following inflections to a word you know might teach you the important concept that words are built up by adding letters.

book	look	go	play
books	looks		plays
	looking	going	playing
	looked		played

Adding letters in front is probably harder.

is	and	am	way
his	sand	Sam	away

Subtracting   Being asked to take letters away from a word you watched your teacher construct in a deliberate way is quite easy *provided you know the word*. Teach the child how to delete or subtract word parts on words he already knows.

Substituting initial consonants   Thinking about substitutions at the front end of the word seems to be harder than thinking about the rhymed ending, especially when there are two or three consonants involved. Approach this carefully as you help a child read his book using a word with a single-consonant onset like 'see' and moving to a two-consonant onset like 'tree'.

see	*way*	*duck*
tree	*play*	*truck*

Making analogies

The next sections deal with using the child's ability to make analogies, relating something he knows to something new, and classing the two things as similar. Teachers need to think hard about a child's substitutions in order to work out what the child is attending to. Often the child is jumping to false conclusions, grouping together things that do not in fact belong together. Sometimes the child is forming a habit of looking at particular features, and in fact this will turn out to be a problem later when he is reading more extended texts.

If the child early in his programme is giving

is	for	*as*
said	for	*this*

it could be that he is attending to the '*s*' without regard to other letters present or the order of letters.

Later in his programme a child may give

do not	for	*down*
no	for	*now*
me	for	*came*

and it seems as if he could be looking for little words in big words, ignoring many important things about words.

So it is risky to try to teach children to use analogy unless you are watching carefully for evidence of what they are actually attending to, and what they are concluding from your demonstrations, or from what they themselves analyse or construct.

Analogies of medium difficulty (See also page 45)

The best words to begin to work with will be ones the child knows and the ones from which the child can already isolate a cluster of letters. In other words, the child already has some notion of a cluster of letters which go together but do not form a word. (It does not matter if this is not a unit that a linguist would recognise like onset, rime, syllable or inflection.) At first use clusters that this particular child knows even if they have no linguistic validity. You can shift to linguistic units later.

The tasks in simple analogies (page 45) can be used with words which have two characteristics: they rhyme *and* they have the same spelling patterns in the rhyme. A more competent child could do some word work with words like *come* and *some* or with *pink*, *sink* and *think*.

Working out new words by analogy

The following task is one which teachers find hard, but when they trial it a few times and choose their words well they find that children catch on to what to do very easily. Children need little explanation of the task, just demonstration. It is as if they are already doing something a bit like this in their heads.

Choose two words the child knows well to get to a third but new word. Use the onset of the first word and rime of the second word to make the third word. For example, the teacher might use *to* and *ball* (words the child already knows) to introduce the new word *tall*.

The teacher quickly writes	*to*	and the child reads it.
The teacher writes	*ball*	and the child reads it.
The teacher writes	*tall*	and the child reads it.

Similarly the teacher might go to the words *play*, *stop*, *stay*. In these examples the teacher has given the child all the information he needs to work with (that is, he does not have to call up anything on his own) and will imply that he use the process of analogy to get to the new word. Children can do this.

Harder analogies

It is harder for the child to work with consonants and rhymes when more letters are involved, and also when the spelling pattern does not have a direct letter-sound correspondence. These are traditionally called the spelling pattern families.

all	*mother*	*bite*	*light*
tall	*brother*	*kite*	*night*

Avoid examples that children are unlikely to encounter

The learning task is that these deletions, substitutions and additions can help the reader and writer in everyday word-solving. Examples of how to find these links with words you know are best taken from words the child clearly does know.

Avoid hard tasks. For example it is hard to interchange two first letters to make two new words.

way   sent   (swop initial letters)   *say   went*

A task like this would be unhelpful and unnecessary.

All the different tasks outlined above can be made easy by having the teacher supply all the letters or words the child needs to work with. They can be increased in difficulty by having the child supply some or all of the letters or words. If the teacher takes too big a step in 'taking words apart while reading' the child will end up juggling his responses and will not have learned how to apply what he knows about words to the problem-solving. It is very easy to confuse Reading Recovery children.

To challenge the now-competent reader and writer even harder tasks can be tried — but do not overdo this. Ask the child to supply the derived examples 'out of his head', that is, do not give him the letters or words to use in getting to the new word. In this case the teacher might say

- Make another word that sounds like that.
- Make another word that looks like that.
- Make another word that ends like that.
- Make another word that starts like that.

Testing for control of letter groups

This can be done quite quickly with the more competent reader/writer. The child is asked to write some word he knows and then he is asked to write another word differing in one letter or letter cluster from the one he has already written. Substitutions of this kind help him problem-solve a word in reading.

This spelling-type activity carried out in writing on a chalkboard or paper is harder than making and breaking at the magnetic board.

A scale of help: From least help to most help
- Let the child solve the word.
- Prompt to the word beginning,
    initial letter, onset, cluster
  or to the ending,
    inflection or rime
  or to any known part.
- The child divides the word with his finger on print or uses a card (mask) in some way.
- The teacher divides the word in print with finger or masking card.
- The teacher writes part of the word on a whiteboard.
- The teacher constructs the word part with magnetic letters.

Cautions Engage in only as much 'taking words apart while reading' as is needed to foster visual analysis of words in the reading books (Section 4). Do not use time on this unless it is clear that the child needs this activity! Talk about words the child knows or is working on; do not use rhymes, or word family examples which have no bearing on this child's current needs for reading this text. Do not do it because it might help in the future; only because it is needed now. And preferably work on the text being read.

Once a child has begun to take words apart during text reading, magnetic letters could be used occasionally while reading text to make a teaching point. Do not allow this activity to make it hard to remember the story so far.

12 TEACHING FOR PHRASING IN FLUENT READING

Introduction

Why is it important to think about phrasing in fluent reading? The answer is simple. When the reading is phrased like spoken language and the responding is fluent (and some people say fast), then there is a fair chance that the reader can read for meaning and check what he reads against his language knowledge. And his attention can go mainly to the messages.

The beginning reader has many things to learn about literacy and a heavy load of new concepts, new ideas, and new language slows the reader down. Also there are many different sources of information in print and the reader has to remember how to get to these and how they will help him. So beginning readers read slowly.

Then on continuous text the processing that the reader has to do is complex: looking for visual information across words, choosing the word, monitoring his own response, relating it to what has gone before, self-correcting if necessary. This all takes time and slows down the responding. The one-to-one matching, with or without pointing, involves rather slow motor (movement) responses; so does moving the eyes across the words and lines, looking for helpful cues.

All these things essentially slow down beginning readers. Studies of speed of reading show how it gets faster as the beginner becomes a competent reader.

Teachers are warned not to make things worse by the ways in which they teach. There are four obvious ways in which teachers can contribute to slow reading (and we could probably think of many more).

1 As the child begins to match what he says with what he sees *his reading should slow down* until he has coordinated speech with looking at print. Then good readers speed up again. Only good observation and good judgement by the teacher will tell her when the child should be encouraged to speed up his responding because his one-to-one matching is secure. This principle recurs throughout these procedures.

In Reading Recovery it is an overriding principle that *as soon as control is firmly established the teacher should begin to call for flexible use of that control*. In this case flexibility means varying the speed of reading to suit the difficulty of the text. It is very easy for children to habituate a slow, staccato, word-by-word habit of reading which is *very hard to break*. Avoid this.

2 A second way to slow down young children's reading is to make them think that reading has only to do with letters, sounds, and words. Overattention to these levels of language will displace, in the child's mind, the idea that there are meaningful stretches of language involved. In Reading Recovery this should never occur. Letter and word work should always seem to the child to be used in the service of text reading or text writing. Keep the balance of attention on language and meaning in continuous text.

3 A third way to slow up children's reading is to interrupt the reading so much with your teaching that it all sounds to the child like a string of unlinked words.

From any one of these three emphases in teaching the child can get the impression that reading is supposed to be carried out slowly word by word, with heavy emphasis on each word, and often in a special 'reading voice'.

Alternatively, a child can learn precisely this by hearing other children who read that way and matching his own behaviour to theirs.

4 There is a fourth way to slow down young readers. If the child talks to himself about his problem-solving—say in forming a letter, or instructing himself to look at the first letter, or to 'sound the word out'—some teachers believe that such self-instruction will be helpful but again this slows down the processing of the information in print at a rate which makes reading easy. Competent readers survive such instruction better than those finding literacy learning difficult.

Another form of this occurs when teachers try to apply what we have learned about metacognition. Because successful readers are able to comment on how they do their problem-solving, some teachers have taught children with difficulties a form of words to use in the hope that this will create in them the skill to do what the words say. That is the wrong way round, to my mind.

So as a result of necessary and unnecessary influences we can have our beginning readers spitting out the words like sausages coming from a sausage-making machine, even though we tried to avoid this. The question then is 'What can we do about it?'

Saying 'Read it fast' will not do

No one can impose fluent reading on the complex processing of continuous text any more than you can make the beginning writer a fast writer. It takes time to develop fast control of many subparts of a complex whole so that it operates smoothly and fluently.

And we may never know what it is that needs to speed up for it is probably different for different children.

Let me try a risky analogy. Suppose you were given the job of running-in a vehicle with 16 gears and you really had no idea what gear changes were possible and what short-cuts could be taken. All you knew was that you had to get this vehicle going in close to top gear. It is pretty obvious that having someone alongside you urging you to speed up is not good enough, is it?

So what do teachers know about what supports fluent reading? They know that

- The oral language of the child is fluent, and it is phrased as language is phrased in normal conversation.
- Thinking is fast and fluent, so meaning helps to link ideas together and group them in memory.
- Seeing or recognising objects is fast and fluent in ordinary life but only when we have become familiar with objects in general and these objects in particular. Recognition becomes faster as visual familiarity increases.
- Orchestrating oral reading with efficient processing of information is fluent when it comes together well and occurs on material that is just challenging enough. To achieve smooth integration of all the processing activities the teacher will sometimes need to drop the difficulty level of text until things are working well. It takes time to learn this smooth orchestration of processing behaviours and tasks should be selected to allow it to occur and then be practised.

Check that oral language, meaning, visual information and text difficulty are all contributing to successful reading. Then try some of the following approaches.

Recovery procedures

Appeal to oral language experience
Encourage the child to read familiar text quickly.

Say '*Can you read this quickly,*'
or '*Put them all together so that it sounds like talking*'.

Especially with direct speech ask the child to read it as he would if he was in that situation. For example, '*I'll eat you up!*'

Demonstrate phrasing on the text

Mask the text with a card or your thumb and expose two or three words at a time asking the child to '*Read it all*.'

Use an overhead projector, masking the text and pacing the child as you expose some for him to read.

Slide a card underneath each line if you wish to discourage word-by-word reading, finger pointing or voice pointing.

Slide a card over the text forcing the child's pace so he processes a little more fluently without breaking down. This encourages him to make his eyes work ahead of his voice.

Insist that the child pause appropriately, especially at full stops and speech marks. Say '*Read the punctuation*.'

Every day in the lesson of the child who is well into his programme and whose fluent reading is being encouraged, take his assembled cut-up story and, in an accepting way, rearrange it into the phrases you think he should use to achieve fluent reading and have him reread it in phrases. This will provide an action demonstration of what phrasing is about, on something he can and does read fluently.

Select texts to facilitate fluent reading

Use known texts, or texts with rhythm-like songs and poems (or sometimes prose) because they carry the reader forward.

Choose repetitive texts which are better read with exaggerated expressions like 'The Greedy Cat'.

Read a story to the child demonstrating fluent reading. Reread it with the child, emphasising the phrasing. This should provide support from the feel and the sound of the patterns of words and breaks or pauses. Write down a repetitive sentence or phrase from a specially selected story and treat it as described for the story above.

In addition to these things

Fluent reading will arise from teacher attention to the role of oral language, and thinking and meaning, and increasing experience with the visual information in print, and practice in orchestrating complex processing on just-difficult-enough texts. It is a matter of successful experience over a period of time moving up a gradient of difficulty of texts which can support fluent and successful reading.

It has quite as much to do with looking as it has to do with language.

---

13 TEACHING FOR A SEQUENCING PROBLEM

Introduction

Although the skilled reader may not attend to cues in print in a strictly left-to-right order, that is how our written code is organised and children have to be able to attend to cues in sequence. Children have difficulty with this for quite different reasons.

- Some find it very difficult to control the steady letter-by-letter analysis sometimes required of them and they adopt a haphazard approach because it is easier.
- Others could exercise the required control but they prefer a more interesting, varied approach and resist the attempt to confine their processing to a more orderly procedure.
- A sequencing problem may be caused by lack of feeling for direction.
- It may be a result of poor checking skills for maintaining consistency.

Recovery procedures

1 Have the child construct a tricky word out of magnetic letters. Say '*Once more, as fast as you can*,' encouraging several attempts to provide practice for doing this fluently.

2 Have the child write a word in an unlined book several times. Say '*Once more, as fast as you can*,' encouraging correct and fluent performance. Write this word in a sentence in an unlined book.

3 Use word making and breaking, forming new words by substitution of single magnetic letters.

4 Practise word-construction letter by letter with word boxes on the blackboard (see discussion on sound segmentation page 32).
   '*What can you hear at the beginning?*'
   '*What can you hear at the end?*'

Articulate carefully letter by letter for the child so that you lengthen the sound of the particular letter he is working on.

Have the child reconstruct a cut-up child-dictated sentence which the teacher has written. Gradually as the child improves direct his attention to finer detail in the following order:

A Phrasing
B Words
C Small segments—obvious syllables, endings, common consonant clusters, vowel-consonant clusters (s – and).

The challenge is to maintain sequence despite the attention to detail.

Have at hand masking cards with windows of various sizes to expose segments or groups of units to be attended to. (This is a visual attending device but can also be used to foster correct sequencing.) Use these on text as the child reads or following a page where a difficulty occurred.

Mask a problem word in text exposing a sound unit at a time, and have the child blend in the correct sequence.

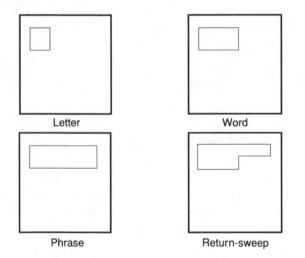

Letter   Word

Phrase   Return-sweep

14 STRONG SKILLS WHICH BLOCK LEARNING

Recovery procedures

If some inappropriate reading skill or responses to a particular item become overlearned and fluent they are hard to unlearn. Some guidelines are:

- Prevent the inappropriate behaviour occurring whenever possible.
- Penetrate the old pattern by splitting it apart—over space and over time.

- Use exaggeration by shouting, by stress, by elaborate acting, by singing in the manner of recitative, and so on.
- Move with large movements before refining the pattern.
- Aim to get flexibility, and alternative operations established.
- Move cautiously towards fluency. The child may manage to control a new response by thinking about it, and although this makes for slow responding, he may then be able to control the old rapid, unthinking, response.

Sometimes children fail to integrate cues from different sources because they tend to focus on one kind of cue ignoring discrepancies in the other types of cue.

As the child reads, his teacher's confirmation of his successful processing and the nature of her prompts become important ways of focusing the child's attention on neglected areas.

What is the teacher's purpose in the questions she uses when she prompts? Probably she has several different kinds of prompts. Sometimes she invites the child to think about meaning as in:

Where do you think the bear lives? (Target word: *cave*)

At other times the prompt may be to check something, like a previous sentence or a rerun of the present sentence:

Perhaps it was sleeping in the...

Another kind of leading question may point the reader towards letter/sound cues, like

'*What sounds can you see in that word?*'

or '*Get your mouth ready for the first sound.*'

And yet another strategy may be to encourage the child to solve the word by analogy with a more frequently used word. This is sometimes difficult, and *cave* is an example of such difficulty.

If a teacher specialises in one type of prompting or cueing the child will tend to specialise (through deprivation of alternative opportunities) and will not achieve flexibility in his use of strategies.

If the child has a bias towards the use of language cues, the teacher's prompts will be directed to either a strong locating response (she may ask him to '*Try that again with your finger*') or to print detail (she may get the child to confirm a prompt by attending to initial and final letters firstly in the spoken word and then in the written word).

15   WHEN IT IS HARD TO REMEMBER

Introduction

Some children have particular difficulty in calling up an association or a label for a word, or a name for a letter or the names for story characters. I refer here to children who have difficulty with recall on most occasions, not merely a temporary lapse. This low recall means that the earliest, easiest and most basic links of oral language with print are very difficult for the child to establish. Some of the following approaches may help.

The teaching goal is to develop strategies for remembering or recalling, rather than merely forcing a particular association into the child's mind.

Recovery procedures

Use the child's association

When Paul knew very few letters he never had difficulty with O. O for Oboe was his association. For him that was easy; for another child it would have been impossible.

Mark had trouble with G. After several weeks his teacher found an appropriate meaningful association that triggered the letter name. By calling part of the symbol a saddle she taught Mark to say '*A saddle for the gee-gee.*' Not the best link for most children but it worked for Mark.

Arrange for repetition

Increase the opportunities to recall, that is, to use strategies for remembering, on a few very important items. Practise recall on known items.

Arrange for overlearning

This refers to the practice we get after something has been learned. It is an insurance against forgetting.

Continue to provide opportunities for further practice long after the labels or names seem to have been learned.

Use games

Sometimes a game like 'Snap' or matching face-down cards is useful for providing both practice and the expectation that one has to remember.

Revise

As a matter of routine go back to old difficulties and check that they have been established by repetition and overlearning. Check these much more carefully than one would have to with most Reading Recovery children.

Teach for flexibility

Use:

- different responses like singing, shouting, or role-playing suitable actions, as for oboe, or gee-gee
- different mediums such as magnetic letters, chalk, felt-tip pens, paint, cards, slide-projection
- and find the items to be remembered in many different locations.

Extend the known set

Have several cards of all the letters/words that the child recognises plus the ones that are half-known plus one or two that have just been taught. Run through these making 'your pile' and 'my pile' of the known and not known words.

Games can be adapted for the purpose of increasing the items that a child remembers. For example, in 'Fishing', the teacher makes several cards of each of the words that the child knows with upper- and lower-case versions. The game is to form pairs by asking your partner if he has a word that you have in your hand.

'Do you have *go*?'
'*Yes*' (he hands it to the teacher) or
'*No—Fish*' (the teacher picks one from the centre pile).

Develop a way of studying words

A child may have some reading skill but may show little skill in accumulating new words or profiting from instruction given only the day before. It is as if he cannot 'hold' the experience, and store it for future use.

Help the child to develop a consistent approach to remembering words. Adapt it to suit the strengths and weaknesses of each child.

- Ask the child to look at the word written on the blackboard or with magnetic letters or in large print. Say it slowly and run your finger across it.
- Ask him to do this.
- Ask him to close his eyes and see it, saying it in parts.
- Ask him to look again, scanning it without help, and saying it in parts. (The problem is probably that he does not search with his eyes the letter outlines, or the letter sequences.)
- Ask him to write it, or parts of it, without looking. (Do not be too strict on this point for young children.) Have him say it as he writes it.

Now present the words in different ways calling for the same responses from the child.

Practise word reconstruction

- Make the word out of magnetic letters. Jumble and remake until the child is fluent.
- Write the word on the blackboard in large print using verbal instructions while writing each letter.

Introduce tracing

If visual analysis and word reconstruction do not produce good results, introduce tracing and add the feel of the movements to the child's sources of information.

- Ask the child to trace the word with finger contact saying the part of the word as he traces it. *Finger contact is important.*
- Repeat this process as often as is necessary until the child can write the word without looking at the copy.
- Write the word on scrap paper as often as is needed to reach fluency.

Other activities

- Encourage the child to include the word in his written story.
- Choose books that include the new word.
- Establish fluency in producing this vocabulary of known words.

A way of remembering

When a child has used these rather laborious strategies for establishing his early visual memories for a small vocabulary of words he usually arrives at the stage where he can take short-cuts.

> '...one of the most interesting things to be found in our non-reading cases (was that) the child, who had to trace each word many times at first, eventually developed the ability to glance over the words of four and five syllables, say them once or twice as he looked at them and then write them without a copy.'
>
> (Fernald, 1943, p. 21 ff.)

The child is then able to learn from the printed word by merely looking at it and saying it to himself before he writes it. He may use one of several strategies—silent articulation, visual scanning or some other aid.

Dale was certain about his visual memory for some words. The teacher said, '*Have a look at "come", a really good look, and then write it down there.*' Dale replied, '*I don't have to look.*' He covered his eyes and wrote the word. But his final comment was interesting. He said, '*Then you aren't looking and your eyes help you.*'

Relating new words to old

If something is completely novel it requires a great deal of effort to learn about it. If we can relate the new item to something we already know it is easier to master.

To make the child an independent reader the teacher must encourage him to search for links between new words and words he already knows.

Word making and breaking activities help to build such habits of search.

Questioning during book reading can also foster a search for relationships.

16   CHILDREN WHO ARE HARD TO ACCELERATE

Introduction

The patterns of progress made by children will be very different from child to child. For hundreds of children in the New Zealand Reading Recovery Programme acceleration is the outcome of sound teaching. As the child gains control of the various components of the reading process the teacher who is observing sensitively begins to realise that a faster pace up through text difficulty levels is possible. (See page 8.) However, for some children and some teachers this does not seem to happen.

There is only one position to take in this case. The programme is not, or has not been, appropriately adapted to the child's needs. It is time to take a close look at possible reasons for this, and colleague comment is what the teacher should seek.

Steps to take

1 First check up on yourself as teacher.

- Have you made some assumptions about the child that could be wrong?
- Are you operating the programme as required?
- Is your programme addressing the child's strengths and weaknesses that were revealed in the Observation Survey?
- Is writing receiving attention? Or *enough* attention?
- Have you taught in such a way that the child has learned to depend on you, and not to take the initiative?

2 Now check up on your records of the child's progress.

- Look at the first Observation Survey, particularly at the low scores. Which parts of the programme would be difficult because of these?
- Look over your Lesson Records and describe what the succession of learning/failing to learn has been in particular areas. What have your records to say about the things that this child has found difficult?

3 Now set about observing the child's behaviour very closely.

- Ask yourself questions about why he might be finding parts of the task difficult.

Take stock of what you have found in these three areas. Reread the appropriate parts of your supporting texts, using the index. Then talk out your problems with some Reading Recovery colleagues.

- You may decide that you have to work out some new ways of getting the child to do the 'reading work' in the areas in which he is opting out. Use all your ingenuity. Ask others to watch you and the child at work and check out what is happening.

In general, when the child is hard to accelerate he is finding some part or parts of the reading process difficult. Often he has learned to do something which is interfering with his progress, and he may have learned it from the way you have been teaching.

Another reason for the child finding it hard is that some important aspect of the reading process has not received attention. It has been left out of the construction of the reading process.

For most children, whatever the problem, it is wise to drop the level of text difficulty, as a first step. This seems in conflict with the aim to accelerate the child. However, it is the *child* who accelerates, and in one sense the teacher merely matches the texts to the child's rate of acceleration. So, starting on easier text, the child will need to orchestrate the whole process in a more satisfactory way before moving off up the difficulty sequence.

The things to check suggested above were:

- your own teaching behaviour
- your analysis of the child's difficulties
- new explanations that might apply
- the intactness of the reading process on easier material
- whether the child's writing behaviour is improving.

You are likely to have some blind spots in these areas and the opinions of colleagues could be most useful for the readjustment of your programme. It has been one of the values of the Inservice Training sessions that teachers have been able to pool their collective wisdom on their most puzzling pupils.

5 | WHEN TO DISCONTINUE TUTORING

TRANSFER OUT OF THE PROGRAMME

This decision must be weighed up very carefully.

Part of the intensive programme in Reading Recovery is the close supervision by the teacher. This is not typical of the usual classroom programme because of the number of children who need attention.

Early in the Reading Recovery programme the teacher must begin to prepare the child for this transfer. She must never do for the child what he could do for himself. She encourages and reinforces independent operating, and problem detection, and problem-solving. Her teaching must defeat a common outcome of remedial programmes which is that they make the pupils dependent on the teacher. Reading Recovery aims to make children independent of the teacher.

Back in the classroom it would be ideal if the child could work on his own, and be confident enough to know when to appeal for help and how to use that help. He needs to be able to continue to increase his control over reading and writing even with a 'not-noticing' teacher.

For these reasons decisions to discontinue should be made very carefully.

Deciding when to discontinue

How can we decide whether a child is ready for discontinuing the individual tutoring? There can be no hard and fast criteria because the aim will be to replace a child in a class group in which he can continue to make progress, and this will differ from child to child and from school to school.

Consultation will be necessary — with the class teacher, and the teacher in charge of the first years in school. Recorded observations of the child's behaviour during a class reading lesson will give important information for decisions about continuing or discontinuing tuition.

Reading Recovery teachers found the following questions helped them to decide whether a child was ready to be discontinued. (See Record Sheet page 108.)

Setting
Is there an appropriate group at his level towards the middle of his present class? Think about the size of the group, the book level at which they are working, their rate of progress, and the teacher's attitude. The child may need to enter the group at a somewhat lower level than he was working on with his Reading Recovery teacher.

Survival
How well will this child survive back in his class? Will he continue to learn from his own efforts? Has he acquired some of the strategies in a self-extending system? What evidence do you have from his reading or writing?

Running Record analysis
Does he read increasingly difficult material always at 90 percent accuracy or above? Does he read (easy) books for pleasure?

Estimate of scores
Do you expect his scores to have improved on the tasks of the survey? What evidence do you have to support this? Where was he weak before? Will he be able to score much higher now?

Observable behaviours to look for at discontinuing

There is no fixed set of strategies nor any required levels of text nor any test score that must be attained to warrant discontinuing. It is essential that the child has a system of strategies which work in such a way that the child learns from his own attempts to read. Some of the things a child ready for discontinuing will be able to do will be these:

- *Directional movement.* The child will have control over this without lapses, or else will be aware of his tendency to lapse and will be able to check on his own behaviour.
- *One-to-one matching.* The child can adopt a controlled one-to-one matching of spoken to written words for checking purposes.

- *Self-monitoring*. The child is checking on himself. This can be seen when an error is noticed but not corrected. It is also observed as the child reassembles a cut-up story.
- *Cross-checking*. The child notices discrepancies in his own responses by cross-checking one kind of information (say, visual) with a different kind of information (such as meaning).
- *Use of multiple cue sources*. On self-correction behaviour it is sometimes clear that the child is using meaning, and structure, and visual cues and a sense of how words are written, trying to achieve a match across all sources of cues.
- *Self-correction*. Effective self-correction follows from using self-monitoring, searching for cues, and cross-checking information. However even unsuccessful attempts at self-correction are indicators that the child is aware these activities can be helpful.

Questions of level

Usually the child ready for discontinuing can read a text which the average child in his second year at school can read. He can write a couple of sentences for his story, requiring only one or two words from the teacher. Check the record of words written independently and the stories he writes, and make sure there has been marked improvement and that a strategy of getting from sounds to letters has developed.

If discontinuing —

As the next step in discontinuing prepare the child and his class teacher for this, perhaps working with the child in his classroom for the last two weeks of his programme.

Then *have the child tested* on the Observation Survey by an independent tester (another teacher for example) and analyse the strengths and weaknesses at this point in time. Compare them with the earlier testing and note the areas in which progress occurred. At this point decide finally to discontinue.

Discuss the child's current status with his class teacher.

Offer to monitor the child's progress, say once every two weeks, then once a month, until you and his teacher are sure that he is continuing to make progress. It may be that you take a Running Record every two weeks on the books the child is reading in his class, and also discuss his progress in writing with the teacher, talking over a particular piece of work.

If not discontinuing —

The teacher and the Reading Recovery team may make a decision such as one of the following:

- The child needs to continue in the full programme.
- The child needs further help in two or three areas where he is still weak, such as text reading, hearing sounds in sequence, taking words apart or constructing words.
- The child needs further help to survive in the class situation.
- The child needs one or two individual text reading sessions each week for motivation, as a check, to gain confidence, or any other reasons.

Set new learning goals. Aim to make the child independent. Continue only as long as necessary. Make new plans for discontinuing, testing only in the critical areas on this occasion.

Follow-up and check-up

Research studies which followed children who had remedial instruction have often reported that progress was not maintained back in the classroom. Research following up Reading Recovery children (see pages 69–72, 77–81) showed that, in general, progress was sustained for most of the children. However, some children made slow progress for a year and then accelerated again while other children began to lag in progress after two years.

The numbers of such children were small but they led us to recommend that Reading Recovery teachers or some other person given this role should:

- monitor progress sensitively over the next three years
- consider promotions carefully (and not overpromote)
- provide further individual help if needed particularly if progress slows.

Although Reading Recovery children perform well in their classes some of them remain at-risk children, easily thrown by life circumstances or poor learning experiences. A refresher course of individual instruction for quite a short period should be most helpful for a 'recovered' child who has begun to slip behind his classmates.

6 THE READING RECOVERY RESEARCH REPORTS

A research programme was undertaken to explore the extent to which it was possible to undercut reading failure in an education system by a programme of early intervention. Eight projects in this research programme are reported here in somewhat abbreviated form for teachers and administrators.

The research question for all of these studies was 'What is possible?' It was not possible in New Zealand at that time to ask how well this programme worked compared with competing programmes since none existed. The only realistic comparison was with **a**) children unable to be given the programme or **b**) other children in the same age cohort and in classroom programmes. After the first year's success the first alternative was judged to be unethical. The second alternative required an unconventional research design which allowed for three aspects of the treatment that other researchers have found to be problematical.

1   Children spend varying lengths of time in treatment, according to need, and new children enter the programme throughout the year. Analysis of results for a particular school year catches up a group who have had less than the required treatment and whose results cannot be 'added to' those who have been in the programme the required time for them.

2   Children who enter Reading Recovery are the lowest achievers in their age cohort in their own school. As the programme aims to bring those children to average levels of achievement it is necessary to test whether this is achieved by having a research design which allows comparison with the age cohort in that school.

3   Several 'relative' criteria are used in Reading Recovery. The children selected are the lowest achievers in their school, and that level may vary from school to school. Similarly, the children cease to receive individual tuition when they have reached average achievement for their age cohort in their school. Such criteria work well for self-managed schools, and despite the variability between schools

found in education systems, but they present some problems for traditional research designs.

Reading Recovery is an intervention designed to function effectively in an education system so these research projects sought answers to questions about what would be possible if one delivered instruction in a different way and the appropriate comparison was to compare the end result with that of ordinary classroom instruction.

Studies reported here are these.

1   The Development Project, 1976–1977
2   The Field Trial Research in 1978
3   The One-Year Follow-up Research, 1979
4   The Replication Study, 1979
5   The Analysis of Lesson Content, 1978
6   The Three-Year Follow-up, 1981
7   National Monitoring, 1984–1988
8   The Reading Recovery Subgroups Study, 1991

1   THE DEVELOPMENT PROJECT, 1976–1977

The aim of the project was to record how teachers worked with children having marked difficulty learning to read, in a one-to-one teaching situation. We aimed to describe the range and variability of reading behaviours shown by the children and the range and variability of the teaching responses made by the teachers. The children had just completed their first year at school.

The project began with a year of detailed observation and record-keeping as I worked with one teacher, and continued in the second year with practitioners, a team of six people — teachers, supervising teachers, reading advisers and senior University students. They agreed to find time to teach two children individually. They agreed to meet once every two weeks to observe each other teach and to discuss procedures and assumptions. Procedures were evolved for observing the teachers at work, using a one-way screen. At these sessions, the team would discuss pupil and teacher responses as they occurred and following the lesson they would challenge the teachers who had demonstrated to explain why they chose a technique, a particular book or a specific progression. They were asked:

- What contributed to a teaching decision?
- How could they justify it?
- What other difficulties or achievements were the procedures related to?
- Why did the children react in this or that way?
- Why did they not move the child more quickly?

During such discussions the implicit assumptions of the teacher had to be explained verbally rather than remaining intuitive hunches. The process of articulating the basis for a teaching decision was always difficult.

A large number of techniques were piloted, observed, discussed, argued over, related to theory, analysed, written up, modified and tried out in various ways, and, most important, many were discarded. Carefully graded sequences within each technique were described. Thus the procedures were derived from the responses of experienced teachers to children as they tried to read and write. The process of refinement continued over the next three years, as several drafts of the teaching procedures were written, discussed and edited by the teachers. The procedures were derived from the practice of teachers who were working with failing children but they were discussed and analysed in relation to current theories of the reading process. Revision of rationales and procedures continues as 'current theories' change and the balance of research evidence shifts.

The six-year-old children who were referred to the programme were diverse in their response to print. No two children had quite the same problems. Children on the same level of text varied in their profiles of test scores. One may conclude therefore that these children read texts of similar difficulty with skills of different strengths. It followed from this that each child's Reading Recovery programme must be designed to suit the responses in his repertoire and so programmes differed from child to child.

Critical evaluation of the results of the development project suggested that the five most important areas to receive attention in the next stage of our project would be:

1 **Organisation** Children probably needed more intensive programmes than two or three lessons each week if they were to move quickly at accelerated rates of progress.

2 **Teaching** The most effective teaching procedures from our records should be gathered together and articulated to provide better guidance for teachers.

3 **Efficient choices** If effective teaching is to occur sound choices must be made about appropriate procedures. It follows that certain procedures are de-emphasised or eliminated from some children's programmes. Decisions not to do certain things in recovery programmes may be very important. This is a somewhat novel concept in the area of reading difficulties. It relates to economical use of the child's learning time.

4 **Conceptualising the goal** The goal of teaching should be a self-extending system, a set of behaviours which lead the child to control more difficult texts merely because he reads them. The important components of a self-extending system are the in-the-head strategies which the child initiates to capture information in the visual and verbal features of the text, or to detect an error that has been made and to find some way of self-correcting it, using past knowledge to solve a novel problem. Teachers in our next stage of developing the treatment should deliberately focus the child's attention on such processing strategies.

5 **Transfer or generalisation** We must think clearly about the process of discontinuing children from tutoring and the ways in which we could ensure continuing progress back in classrooms. It is not a contradiction to say that we needed to become specific about such generalisation.

2 THE FIELD TRIAL RESEARCH IN 1978

The Field Trial research was an exploratory study to find out what kinds of outcomes were possible.

This study reports the results of the first year of working in schools, the first year of developing the teacher training, and the teaching was being done by teachers who were in training. We had observed good teachers of problem readers working in one-to-one situations, and we had observed the children. We had articulated what we thought were some of the children's problems, and what seemed to be efficient and economical teaching procedures.

The next step was to demonstrate that these procedures worked and that children made progress. However if an early intervention programme were to be adopted in schools we also had to demonstrate that our procedures could work in different school settings. Such evidence would be most important for New Zealand educators who are traditionally very sceptical about the contribution that academics and researchers can make to effective teaching. In addition we would somehow have to find convincing evidence to support the argument for one-to-one teaching, for which there was no precedent in the system.

The research questions in 1978

1   The practical questions concerned how the programme could be implemented in schools.
   *   Could experienced teachers without specialist training use the procedures effectively?
   *   How would the programmes need to vary from school to school?

The plan of operation must allow for teachers to differ, for schools to differ, and the children in different schools to differ. How teachers worked, how many children they took each day or week, and what timetables they derived were not predetermined. Teachers discussed their ideas on these matters with the research staff. Consultation, not prescription, was the key word. We wanted to see what organisation teachers would evolve for mounting the programme in their schools.

2   The other questions concerned what reading progress could be made.
   *   To what extent could the poorest readers be helped by individual tutoring?
   *   How many could be helped?
   *   What were the outcomes of the programme for the tutored children in comparison with the untutored?
   *   Could the gains made in tutoring be sustained after withdrawal of the supplementary tutoring?

The schools

The schools were different in size, in type of organisation,* in population and location. All were in the suburbs of a large metropolitan area. School **A** was a small school in an older state-housing area with some solo parents. School **B** was in a mixed working- and middle-class suburb. School **C** was on the edge of both a middle-class and a working-class new housing area and was the biggest school. In School **D** the children were predominantly from working-class backgrounds with much movement in and out of the school. School **E** was a larger school in a newer state-housing area with 60 percent of the children

---

* Two were open-plan and three had single-cell classrooms.

having solo parents. Auckland schools have high proportions of Maori and Pacific Island children.

The teachers

Principals in those five schools were asked to use the allocated extra teacher to release an experienced teacher of beginning reading who volunteered to do this Reading Recovery training. The teachers released had from five to 12 years' experience. Academic background was not a requirement. All the teachers had been trained in Teachers' Colleges and did not have University Diplomas or degrees. The conditions of a school's participation in the research study were:

*   that the teacher be allowed to test *every six-year-old* within two weeks of his/her birthday
*   that she arrange a programme of individual tutoring for suitable children
*   that her participation in this programme would not be interrupted for any reason (such as relieving, sports duties and school trips).

Testing every child after one year of instruction

To allow for comparison of the children who received help with their classmates who did not, the total age cohort was tested in the five schools. The dates of testing, linked to sixth birthdays, were scattered throughout the year for children whose birthdays fell between 1 September 1977 and 30 September 1978. The mean age of the 291 children at initial testing was six years 1.5 months because testing which began in February 1978 included children born in the previous September. Children who transferred into the schools later in the year were tested if they belonged to the same age cohort.

Who was tutored?

From the 291 children in the age cohort in five schools 122 were given special help.

How children were distributed on the reading books after one year of school differed markedly from school to school. Two main reasons for this were **a**) that the children entering schools differed in background experience and ability from school to school and **b**) that schools paced the introduction of the reading programme differently. Some schools began book reading early and pushed ahead rather rapidly. Others took a longer time to establish foundation skills. Therefore children selected for individual tutoring were not chosen by setting a particular attainment level. *They were selected by the relative crite-rion of being the lowest scorers on text reading in that particular school.* The lowest scorers in School **C** might have scores as high as the average scorers in School **E**. It was not the point of this study to raise all children's performance above a particular level. The teacher available in each school was trying to *raise the performance of the low-progress readers in that school*.

The working hours of the teacher set limits to how many children she could take into her programme. The responsiveness of children to individual teaching determined the number of weeks a child remained in the study. Factors which tended to lengthen time in the programme were language problems, family mobility, unsettled family circumstances, sickness and/or absence, general retardation, and unusual learning problems.

The proportion of the age-cohort who were individually tutored in this field trial year differed from school to school because each school, irrespective of size, was allocated a full-time teacher.

The tutoring programme

Children received individual daily teaching by selected teachers who were undergoing a year's inservice training. Training sessions were held every two weeks. This allowed quality control over the teaching on the one hand, but, on the other hand, the teachers were apprentices, learning how to implement the programme and coming to grips with the decision-making it called for.

The teacher who had completed an Observation Survey Summary Sheet Report* had on hand an analysis of behaviours which should relate directly to her teaching programme.

A typical teaching session included a particular set of activities (see page 14). These placed the emphasis on using text for most of the lesson. As the goal of the programme was to return children to average reading groups in their classrooms it was necessary to accelerate their progress to achieve this. Accelerated progress would be most likely to be achieved if:

- the child had many opportunities to read and write
- the tasks were the same as the ones on which improvement was required, i.e., reading messages and writing sentences
- the child was building a complex, flexible system of alternative responses (Clay, 1991a).

---

* At the time of this research the *Diagnostic Survey* was used (Clay, 1979). This was renamed the *Observation Survey* (Clay, 1993).

When skills are taught in isolation more time must be spent in learning to combine these, and more difficulty is experienced with switching to alternative responses. This slows down learning.

The teacher arranged to see children on a timetable that suited her and the school. Sometimes this was once a day and sometimes twice a day for two sessions (see Table 1). Occasionally towards the end of their programme children would come to her in twos and threes but most of the teaching was done in an individual programme which supplemented the work of the classroom.

The teacher training

The teachers were being trained throughout the year. At first the teachers were encouraged to draw on their past experience. Gradually Reading Recovery procedures were introduced and demonstrated, and teachers were encouraged to change their concept of the task. Every two weeks one of the five teachers would demonstrate by teaching one of her pupils while the other teachers observed and discussed the procedures on the other side of a one-way screen.

Topics raised by the teachers in these discussions seemed to suggest that their attention to the reading process was shifting:

- from teaching for items of knowledge (letters known, words remembered) and getting the child to habituate a skill or memorise a new element
- to developing in the child the willingness to use a variety of text-solving strategies.

Another feature of the shift was away from having the 'poor reader' dependent on the teacher and towards teaching in such a way that the child had many opportunities to teach himself something.

Records

Teachers were encouraged to keep a diary or log book as a personal history of the year's work. Personal reactions and queries were to be dated and entered on both teacher behaviours and perceptions, and child behaviours. In addition each teacher kept the following records on individual pupils.

- An Observation Survey Summary Sheet Report was prepared for each child when he was accepted into the project.
- A Lesson Record was kept for each session with the child, detailing at what point in the teaching sequence

the teacher was working and how the child responded. This provided a record of the small step gains made by each child, and of the progressions which the teacher selected from the teachers' handbook or manual.

- One Running Record of text reading was usually kept for each session.
- A graph of progress by Book Level was plotted from one Running Record each week.

Contact with parents

We hoped schools would feel free to approach parents in whatever would be their normal procedure. In fact, contacts during this first year were minimal.

The discontinuing of tutoring

When the teachers judged from the children's work that they would be able to work with and survive in an appropriate group in their classroom and maintain their progress they recommended the child for discontinuing.

At this point, to provide an objective check on the teacher's estimate of progress, an independent tester read-ministered the Observation Survey. In most cases when a comparison was made with the entry test scores, progress in all tests and on text reading was noted and individual tutoring was discontinued. Sometimes a recommendation was made to continue intermittent lessons to support a child or give further instruction in specific areas of weakness. Occasionally a child was not ready to be discontinued. In most cases the teachers were conservative in their recommendations for discontinuing and had carried the children for longer and to higher levels than we had expected. New children entered individual tutoring throughout the year as others were discontinued.

Testing at the end of 1978

In the last two months of 1978 all children in the age cohort in the five schools were retested by two independent testers. Book Level and Reading Vocabulary were used as two measures of general reading progress.

1 Book Level (Running Records)

The most relevant measure for demonstrating progress was Book Level because it assessed the child's management of problem-solving on continuous text. A scale of difficulty was provided by two Caption Book steps, 24 steps for the basic reading series* plus three paragraphs (2, 3 and 4) from the Neale Analysis of Reading Ability (1958), making 29 steps. The highest level on the scale that a child could attempt with 90 percent (or above) accuracy determined his score. This type of measure had proved to be a valid and reliable test of reading progress in other research (Clay, 1966; Robinson, 1973; Wade, 1978). It is not an equal interval scale.

2 Reading Vocabulary

A standardised test was also used. Previous research with children of this age in New Zealand schools (Clay, 1966) had shown that low-progress children could be given the Word Test and high-progress children could be given the Schonell R1 test and that a satisfactory measure *for research purposes* was obtained by combining these two scores. This procedure was used again in this study and the combined scores for Reading Vocabulary yielded a normal distribution. A Word Test score provides only a sign or indicator of reading progress, because the test behaviour that is scored does not involve management of the behaviours needed to read continuous text.

* The New Zealand 'Ready to Read' series (1963).

Table 1	Organisation differences in five schools				
	Number of children in tuition	**Mean weeks in programme**		**Mean length of lessons (in minutes)**	**Mean number of lessons**
		Discontinued	**Not Discontinued**		
A[1]	22	15.1	12.0	40.5	27.6
B[2]	28	11.3	11.8	40.0	21.8
C	22	11.6	13.0	35.9	33.8
D	29	13.2	13.8	26.7[3]	33.3
E[1], E[2]	21	16.2	15.1	40.0	26.4
Average		14.0	13.1		

1 These schools had women principals, the others had men.
2 These schools had open plan organisation for junior classes.
3 Mean length of lesson was affected by some use of group instruction.

The other tests used were from the Observation Survey: Concepts About Print (CAP), Letter Identification (LI), Writing Vocabulary (WV), Dictation Test (DIC), (Clay, 1979; see also Clay, 1993).

Scores on these tests were interpreted as indicators of some component reading skills covering directional and visual discrimination learning (CAP), letter identity (LI), a writing vocabulary of words known in every detail (WV) and sound-to-letter association (DIC).

Results: organisational factors

How did teachers adapt this opportunity for individual instruction to the setting of their particular school?

Numbers and sex of children

The number of children who received tuition from teachers ranged from 20 to 30 per teacher per year working full-time (Table 1). 61 percent of the children tutored were boys and 39 percent were girls.

Weeks in programme

Table 1 shows the average pattern, and individual school averages, for time in tuition. There was an average lag of three to five weeks between sixth birthday and entry to the programme, for a variety of unavoidable reasons such as vacations, a full tutoring roll, a need for testing to be scheduled and/or absences.

The average length of individual programmes was 13 to 14 weeks. It should be stressed that this was an *average* length of time in tuition; individual children needed more time in the programme.

Length of lessons

The arrangements that teachers made for lessons varied from child to child and from teacher to teacher. Three teachers used a 40-minute lesson most of the time and others used a short and a long lesson, one of 30 minutes and a second of 10 minutes later in the day (Table 1).

Results: progress of the children

The progress of the three groups will be reported - the Control group, the Discontinued group and the Not Discontinued group. Readers will recall that new children entered the programme throughout the year.*

---

* On the average five teachers taught and discontinued eight children, then taught and discontinued another eight, and then admitted a further seven children who had incomplete programmes at the end of the school year. Seven children did not benefit from the programme.

Control group   The 160 children not selected for tutoring (who were of the same age group, attended the same schools and had higher initial attainment), were used as a reference group for the tutored children. (Table 2 footnote.)

Discontinued   Children who were tutored and discontinued during the school year had been back in the class programme for an average of 12 weeks (N = 53). Another discontinued group were those who were receiving tuition up until the time of final testing and who met the criteria used to discontinue children (N = 27). These two subgroups make up the Discontinued group.

Not Discontinued   These were children who were receiving tuition at the time of final testing and needed further instruction (N = 42). They had entered the programme as others left it and their programmes were incomplete.

Within-group changes

The mean test scores of all three groups (Discontinued, Not Discontinued and Control) increased from initial to final testing on Book Level, Reading Vocabulary, Concepts About Print, Dictation, and Letter Identification so that statistically significant differences were recorded (see Table 2). Writing Vocabulary was not administered initially to the Control group, but significant differences were found for both tutored groups.

Figure 1 shows the progress of the three groups on Book Level at initial and final testing. The Reading Vocabulary Test graph (not shown) plotted a similar shift. Despite the very different nature of these measures, one measuring accuracy on text and the other word reading in isolation, the type of change for each group was similar.

The movement of the Discontinued group from low-level scoring to average levels is visually apparent and the fact that the Not Discontinued group need further tuition can also be noted.

A third way of reporting the progress was with the gains in Stanine scores. These are reported in Table 3 and Figure 2 (page 68).

The pupils who received individual tuition made gains which equalled or exceeded the gain scores made by their classmates who showed initially the higher achievement. The following statements refer to *the number of Stanines gained* but they do not imply that the groups were scoring at the same level on the tests.

a   The Discontinued group made higher and significantly different gains from the Control group in all tests. (Writing Vocabulary was not administered initially to the Control group.) (Table 3 and Figure 2.)

TABLE 2	Initial and Final test scores							
Test	Group	Test time	N	Mean	SD	Sm	t-test[1] of differences	Correlation of Initial and Final test
Book Level	Discontinued	1	80	6.33	3.67	0.41	25.80	0.53*
		2	80	18.53	3.96	0.44		
	Not Discontinued	1	42	2.48	1.61	0.25	15.12	0.48*
		2	42	8.21	2.76	0.43		
	Control [2]	1	160	12.54	5.86	0.46	22.12	0.64*
		2	160	20.86	5.47	0.43		
Reading Vocabulary	Discontinued	1	80	9.25	9.32	1.04	4.09	0.42*
		2	80	27.63	6.46	0.72		
	Not Discontinued	1	42	4.76	2.96*	0.46	12.28	0.47*
		2	42	14.76	5.20	0.80		
	Control	1	160	24.03	16.78	1.33	19.18	0.74*
		2	160	33.53	11.51	0.91		
Concepts About Print	Discontinued	1	80	13.86	2.78	0.31	18.14	0.35*
		2	80	19.79	2.34	0.26		
	Not Discontinued	1	42	10.90	2.89	0.45	16.05	0.71*
		2	42	16.00	2.45	0.38		
	Control	1	160	16.83	3.43	0.27	5.73	0.64*
		2	160	17.41	3.77	0.30		
Letter Identification	Discontinued	1	80	37.20	13.52	1.51	9.92	0.14
		2	80	51.55	3.20	0.36		
	Not Discontinued	1	42	23.67	14.39	2.22	12.78	0.72*
		2	42	43.29	9.59	1.48		
	Control	1	160	49.86	8.67	0.69	3.91	0.55*
		2	160	50.74	6.30	0.50		
Writing Vocabulary	Discontinued	1	80	10.38	5.80	0.65	17.67	0.18
		2	80	45.69	12.24	1.59		
	Not Discontinued	1	42	5.64	2.90	0.45	14.92	0.47*
		2	42	24.05	9.21	1.42		
	Control	1		(Not administered)				
		2	160	48.19	21.76	1.72		
Dictation	Discontinued	1	80	15.44	7.83	0.88	21.39	0.31*
		2	80	33.24	2.97	0.33		
	Not Discontinued	1	42	8.29	7.31	1.13	17.31	0.62*
		2	42	24.52	6.53	1.01		
	Control	1	160	27.70	8.59	0.68	6.50	0.65*
		2	160	32.96	5.82	0.46		

1 All t-tests are above 2.69 and are significant.
2 This should be called a comparison or reference group because it was not a randomly assigned group. It was a group deliberately chosen to show the outcome achievements of the treated group in relation to their average and better peers.
* Correlations that were significantly above zero at the p < 0.01 level have an asterisk.

b The Not Discontinued group made gains that were not significantly lower than those of the Control group on Book Level, Reading Vocabulary and Letter Identification. They were significantly higher on Concepts About Print and Dictation.

c The Discontinued group made significantly higher gains than the Not Discontinued pupils on Writing Vocabulary.

The only children in the age cohort (282) for whom the programme was insufficient or unsuitable, were:

- four Pacific Island children with insufficient English to understand the instructions of the Observation Survey (and presumably the instructional programmes). Many Pacific Island children made satisfactory progress in the programme.

- one Indian child with flaccid cerebral palsy who made little progress and who was referred to the Psychological Service.

- two children who were helped in the programme but were also seen by the Psychological Service as possibly needing placement in special classes for children of low intelligence.

The Field Trial study results surprised us. High numbers of children were discontinued, the third intake of children had incomplete programmes and only seven children had to be referred for specialist reports and continuing help.

Further comment on the Field Trial phase has been made in the one-year follow-up research (next section).

FIGURE 1   Progress of three groups on Book Level at Initial and Final testing.

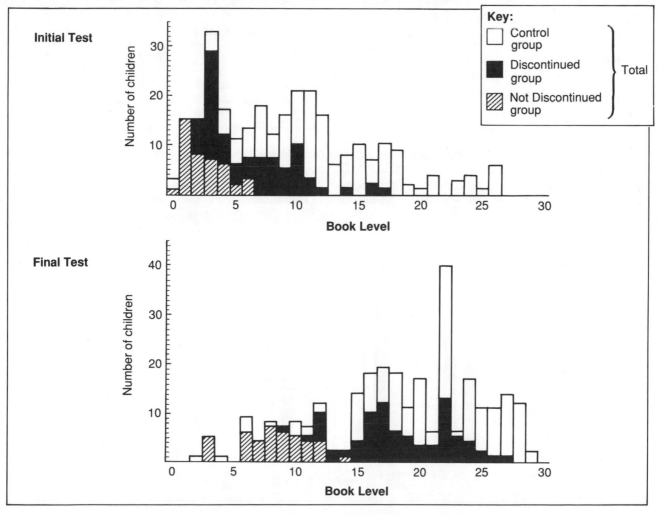

TABLE 3	Gain scores for all measures (with t-tests for significant differences between groups)						
Test	Group	N	Mean	SD	SE$_m$		t$_1$
Book Level	Discontinued	80	2.84	1.13	0.13		4.62*
	Not Discontinued	42	2.00	0.80	0.22		
	Control	160	2.06	1.20	1.11		0.29
Reading Vocabulary	Discontinued	80	2.76	1.01	0.11		5.30*
	Not Discontinued	42	1.69	0.87	0.13		
	Control	160	1.89	1.23	0.11		0.94
Concepts About Print	Discontinued	80	2.99	1.51	0.17		9.65*
	Not Discontinued	42	2.14	1.00	0.15		
	Control	160	1.19	1.14	0.13		4.83*
Letter Identification	Discontinued	80	2.33	1.36	0.15		5.47*
	Not Discontinued	42	1.83	0.93	0.14		
	Control	160	1.34	1.17	0.11		2.45
Writing Vocabulary	Discontinued	80	4.15	1.28	0.14		9.06*
	Not Discontinued	42	2.00	1.17	0.18		
	Control	(Not administered)					
Dictation	Discontinued	80	2.71	1.14	0.13		8.29*
	Not Discontinued	42	2.14	0.95	0.15		
	Control	160	1.38	1.11	0.10		3.99*

*   t-test indicates a significant difference between groups.

FIGURE 2   Gains in Stanine scores in Discontinued, Not Discontinued and Control groups.

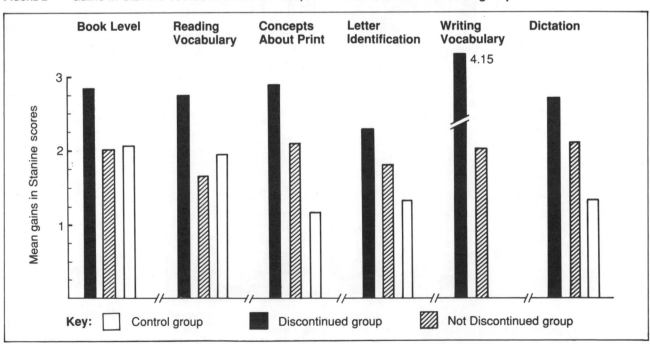

3 THE ONE-YEAR FOLLOW-UP RESEARCH, 1979

One year later the progress of all these children was reassessed. Many things could have upset any trends established by tutoring in the previous year. Control children might forge ahead at a faster rate once the early skills had been mastered as they profited from wide-ranging individual reading. Discontinued children might be unable to build on their gains and so slip back. Not Discontinued children might have slipped further behind or they might have been able to accelerate their progress. No further individual help had been provided during this year.

The research questions

Questions for the one-year follow-up study were:

- What gains were made in 1979?
- Was the relative status of the groups maintained?
- Were gains made during tutoring sufficient to allow children to progress with their average classmates?
- Were the gains made better than those predicted by the statistical phenomenon of regression to the mean?

The research phases

This description of phases is necessary for the interpretation of the tables and figures in this section.

The children entered school on their fifth birthdays and were tested one year later, on their sixth birthdays. As this birthday occurred anywhere between September 1977 and September 1978 the first phase began for individual children at variable dates throughout the year.

The tutoring phase (Phase 1) The tutoring phase began soon after a child's sixth birthday and continued as long as necessary to meet preset criteria of performance based on reading strategies. On average a period of 13 to 14 weeks was needed. Children were discharged from tutoring when they demonstrated a set of behaviours thought to be related to surviving in the ordinary classroom programme. If children did not demonstrate these behaviours they continued in the programme. Of necessity the tutoring phase ended for all children at the end of the school year, December 1978.

Back-in-class phase (Phase 2) The decisions about discontinuing tutoring and the staggered timing of the children's entry into the tutoring phase created a group of children who had a period back in their classroom after tutoring and before the end of the school year.

The follow-up phase (Phase 3) No contact was made with the children during 1979. Some moved to new schools. In December 1979 all children who could be located in the Auckland area were retested by trained testers not associated with the programme. Of the 291 children originally tested in five schools at six years 282 were retested in December 1978 (97%) and 270 in December 1979 (93%). Numbers in the groups at follow-up were Control 153 (160), Discontinued 76 (80), Not Discontinued 41 (42). The losses were low in number and spread across the groups.

		Mean			SD		
TABLE 4	**Mean scores for research groups on Book Level and Reading Vocabulary**						
Test	Group	6:0	1978[1]	1979[1]	6:0	1978[1]	1979[1]
Book Level	Total	9.40	18.51	24.39	6.22	6.42	4.92
	Control	12.54	20.86	26.36 ⎤ *	5.86	5.47	3.29
	Discontinued	6.33	18.53	24.66 ⎦	3.67	3.96	3.10
	Not Discontinued	2.48	8.21	16.23 ⎦ *	1.61	2.76	4.75
Reading Vocabulary	Total	16.20	28.86	41.52	10.40	11.29	13.13
	Control	24.03	33.53	47.07 ⎤ *	16.78	11.51	12.11
	Discontinued	9.25	27.63	39.09 ⎦	9.32	6.46	7.36
	Not Discontinued	4.76	14.76	24.59 ⎦ *	2.96	5.20	8.99

1 End of year.
* Differences are significant at $p < 0.01$ level.

FIGURE 3   **Mean scores for Reading Vocabulary at Initial, Discontinuing, Final and Follow-up testing for Control, Discontinued and Not Discontinued groups.**

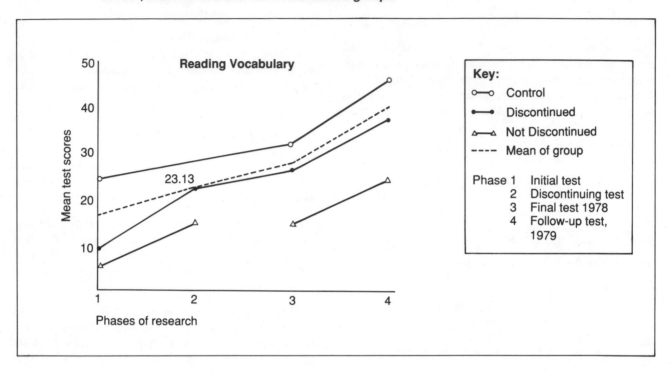

FIGURE 4   **Mean scores for Book Level at Initial, Discontinuing, Final and Follow-up testing for Control, Discontinued and Not Discontinued groups.**

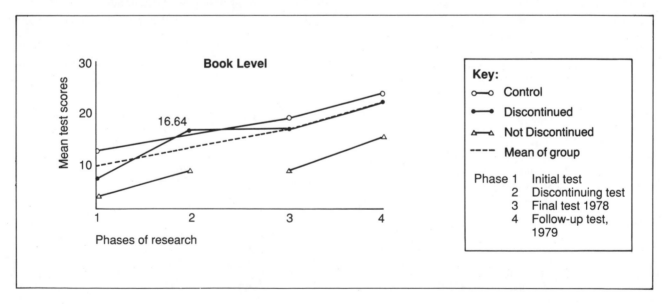

Table 5	Correlations between Initial scores and Final scores (3–11 months) and Follow-up scores (15–23 months)				
	Time	Control	Discontinued	Not Discontinued	Total
Book Level	Final	0.64	0.54	0.48	
	Follow-up	0.50	0.30	0.48	0.61
Reading Vocabulary	Final	0.74	0.42	0.47	
	Follow-up	0.63	0.20	0.50	0.71

Results

Table 4 and Figures 3 and 4 summarise the comparisons at Initial, Final and Follow-up testing for the total group and each subgroup. Mean scores rose during Reading Recovery instruction for tutored groups and gains continued in the following year at a satisfactory level.

The Control group scored above the mean of the total group at each of three testing times (Initial, Final and Follow-up) on two test variables, Book Level and Reading Vocabulary.

The Discontinued group of children had low Initial scores. Final scores were well within one standard deviation of the Control group's Final means, and they retained that position at Follow-up testing. It would be reasonable to claim that children in that position should be able to profit from the usual classroom instruction. This applied to both the Book Level and Reading Vocabulary measures.

For the Discontinued group the correlations of Initial scores with Final and Follow-up scores were lower, as one would predict following this intervention programme (Table 5).

For the Not Discontinued group the correlations of Initial scores with Final and Follow-up scores were higher than for the Discontinued group (they were not so influenced by the programme) but lower than those of the Control group (Table 5).

Do Initial scores predict Final and Follow-up scores?

To answer this question steps were taken that would take account of a regression to the mean effect. Pupils who score lowest tend to make the greatest gains on a second testing. It was necessary to show that any movement of the children with low reading attainment towards the mean of the group was greater than would be predicted by a regression effect. The correlation between two sets of scores for the total group was used to establish a predicted Final, and a predicted Follow-up score for each value in the scale of scores. For every child a difference score was calculated between **a)** the predicted Final and the actual Final score and **b)** the predicted Follow-up and the actual Follow-up score. Mean difference scores for Control, Discontinued and Not Discontinued groups were compared by t-tests.

The results in Table 6 show that for Book Level and Reading Vocabulary the Control group were close to predicted scores on each variable, and on both occasions. The Discontinued children were consistently higher than would be predicted, i.e., their gains were greater than would be predicted by regression effects on each variable and on both occasions. The Not Discontinued children were consistently lower than would be predicted on each variable and on both occasions.

The results of the t-tests between the mean difference scores for groups show that the Discontinued group made

Table 6	Mean difference scores between predicted N_1 and Follow-up N_2 scores for Book Level and Reading Vocabulary**					
			Book Level		Reading Vocabulary	
Group	N_1	N_2	Final	Follow-up	Final	Follow-up
Control	160	153	0.14	0.44	0.94	0.45
Discontinued	80	76	2.34 ⏋*	1.66 ⏋*	2.26 ⏋*	2.33 ⏋
Not Discontinued	42	41	− 5.02 ⏌*	− 4.84 ⏌*	− 6.56 ⏌	− 6.36 ⏌ *

*	t-tests yield significant differences at the p<0.01 level.
**	A difference score of 0.00 represents no difference from the predicted score. Plus scores are higher than predicted; minus scores are lower.

TABLE 7	Follow-up test scores for children who transferred into research schools		
	N	Book Level	Reading Vocabulary
Control	153	26.36	47.07
Discontinued	76	24.66	39.09
Not Discontinued	41	16.44	24.59
Transfers *	36	21.44	36.11
Total (without transfers)	270	24.39	41.52

significantly better progress than the Control group relative to their Initial scores, and this trend was maintained at Follow-up. The Discontinued group made significantly better progress than the Not Discontinued group relative to their Initial scores and this trend was maintained at Follow-up.

In summary, the results support the interpretation that the children who were tutored until it was judged that they could survive in their classrooms were at Follow-up one year later scoring above predicted scores while the children with incomplete programmes who were judged not to be ready for the termination of their individual tutoring programme were in every comparison below predicted scores. This is taken to be support for two theoretical arguments. The first is that the operational criteria used for judging that children were using certain processing strategies while reading were successful in separating out two groups of children. The second is that the theory upon which the instructional programme was based (that gains in reading can be described in terms of operations carried out by children rather than items of knowledge gained) has received endorsement since discontinuing judgements were made on the evidence of strategic behaviour.

The need to complete Reading Recovery programmes in the following school year for the incomplete group was now clearly evident because after their incomplete programmes these children did not spontaneously shift into the average group.

---

* Supplementary analysis: the transfer group

During the Follow-up Phase when no Reading Recovery programme was available to the schools, 36 children of the same age cohort transferred into the research schools. They were tested at Follow-up as a group who had not been in contact with the Reading Recovery programme. Their scores on four test variables were significantly lower than those of the total group, and lower than the Discontinued group (see Table 7) but higher than those of the Not Discontinued group. The gains of the Discontinued group showed a level of achievement one year later, higher than that of all children who had changed schools, a group which would include competent, average and poor achievement children.

4   THE REPLICATION STUDY, 1979

An inservice course in 1979 trained new teachers in the operation of Reading Recovery programmes in 48 schools. These teachers worked at individual teaching for 10 hours a week, a considerable reduction on the 25 hours available in the 1978 field trial schools. Consequently the 1979 teachers taught and discontinued fewer children per teacher and lesson time was reduced from 40 to 30 minutes. Because they taught fewer children and yet selected the poorest in their schools, the children were, as a group, more challenging and difficult than those taught in the field trials. A class teacher in each school was trained to carry out the final testing to provide for independent assessment.

The research question

The research question was 'Under such changed conditions how well would three new groups of teachers perform in comparison with the five field trial teachers in 1978?'

Could the results of the first year be replicated by a large number of teachers in a large number of schools?

Procedures

The 48 schools which had teachers in training in 1979 were listed alphabetically and divided into three groups (B, C, D) providing three replication samples. The average levels of scoring for the 1979 groups (B, C, D) were compared with the 1978 field trials results (called Group A).

Results

In Table 8 and Figure 5 'Dis' refers to children discontinued with Phase 2 (see page 69), 'Dd' refers to children discontinued without Phase 2, and 'Not Dis' refers to those not ready to be discontinued because of less than complete programmes.

FIGURE 5   **Reading Vocabulary, Book Level, Writing Vocabulary and Dictation scores for four samples: A (1978), B, C, D (1979). Mean scores of Initial (1), Discontinuing (2) and Final (3) tests.**

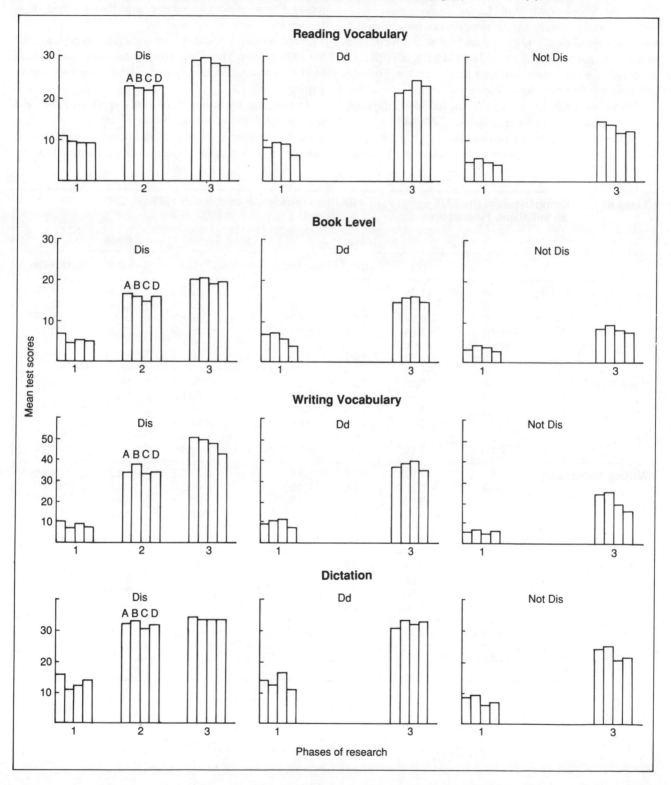

The Initial and Final scores for the four samples in Table 8 cluster within a narrow range. Results for Concepts About Print and Letter Identification tests yielded similar results. It is possible to conclude that teachers guided by a year-long inservice course were able to replicate the results of the 1978 field trials in regard to the level of most scores although they were not working full-time and therefore helped fewer children.

F-tests for each set of scores suggest the following qualifications to the above conclusion (Table 8).

Children taken into the programme in 1979 (samples B, C, D) had lower scores on entry in Reading Vocabulary and Book Level but similar final scores compared with the 1978 sample. Teachers presumably retained them in the programme until they reached satisfactory levels of performance.

Final Writing Vocabulary scores tended to be lower for the 1979 groups. There is a strong possibility that teachers in 1979 with less tutoring time available gave less time to writing.

Overall the results in 1979 fairly replicated the field trials of 1978 and variations between samples were small. Time for tutoring emerged as an important variable and lower entry scores imply more individual tutoring time.

TABLE 8	Comparison of the 1978 sample (A) with three replication samples in 1979 (B, C, D) on Initial and Final scores						
		Initial			Final		
		Dis	**Dd**	**Not Dis**	**Dis**	**Dd**	**Not Dis**
Reading Vocabulary	A	11.79	8.15	4.76	29.54	22.19	14.76
	B	8.39	9.53	5.85	29.98	22.42	13.73
	C	8.71	9.50	4.62	28.52	24.65	11.90
	D	8.65	6.71	4.38	28.29	23.13	12.16
	F ratios	3.87*	1.22	0.92	0.74	1.16	1.68
Book Level	A	6.94	5.07	2.48	20.17	15.04	8.21
	B	4.69	6.78	4.02	20.52	16.89	9.31
	C	5.19	7.15	2.82	19.29	17.15	8.03
	D	5.14	4.13	2.25	19.51	15.00	7.75
	F ratios	3.46*	2.91	4.67**	1.59	3.34*	1.12
Writing Vocabulary	A	11.02	9.11	5.64	51.02	39.96	24.05
	B	8.63	10.26	7.05	49.56	38.74	25.07
	C	9.08	11.55	5.15	48.10	39.10	18.77
	D	8.67	7.88	5.43	42.79	35.21	16.66
	F ratios	2.09	1.38	1.48	2.87*	0.81	4.62**
Dictation	A	16.25	13.89	8.29	34.38	31.07	24.52
	B	11.58	12.74	9.33	33.73	33.63	25.40
	C	12.65	14.90	5.61	33.63	32.85	20.72
	D	13.00	11.29	6.50	33.65	32.96	21.81
	F ratios	3.19*	0.61	2.71	0.68	2.91	2.59

*   Differences significant at $p < 0.05$ level.
** Differences significant at $p < 0.01$ level.

5 THE ANALYSIS OF LESSON CONTENT, 1978
Marie M. Clay and Barbara Watson

It is important for policy-makers and researchers to know whether a programme can be delivered as designed.

In November 1981 the Department of Education approved a research grant for the retrospective analysis of the records of children who were in the Reading Recovery field trials in 1978. Teachers had been required to keep detailed notes of exactly what occurred in each individual lesson. An evaluation of the programmes delivered was made from the analysis of those records.

Finding the children

The 122 children taught during the field trials of the Reading Recovery project in 1978 were traced in December 1981. A letter to each school brought quick returns listing the children still attending or providing the name of the next school attended. All the children were traced. Six were not available for retesting as they had left the Auckland area. This was a high retention rate after three years.

Ethnic group membership

In 1978 we did not know what ethnic groups the Reading Recovery children belonged to. In December 1981 a research assistant visited each school to make detailed enquiries about ethnic group membership. Teaching, clerical, nursing, caretaking staff and parent helpers supplied information and the children themselves or siblings were occasionally consulted. The information included:

- all the information about the ethnic group membership of any one child, allowing for one, two or more than two group affiliations

- the kind of evidence that informants were using to arrive at their judgements
- the roles of people providing the information.

Decisions were made about the quality of this information and a classification of 'Not Known' was used if these sources produced inconsistent, unreliable or insufficient information. An approach to the children's parents did not seem justified for what was a case-file reanalysis study, although we recognised that the parents would provide the most valid information.

On this information we excluded five of the 52 Maori or Pacific Island children (three children for whom we had insufficient evidence, one part-Maori child with a very high proportion of European ancestry, and one adopted child). The six children who now lived outside the Auckland District were all Polynesian (Maori or Pacific Island children), and one further child from these groups was absent from school throughout the retesting period. This reduced the available sample of Polynesian children to 40. Children who had fewer than 15 lessons were also excluded because it was decided to set a lower limit to the time spent in the programme. This resulted in the loss of a further six children, reducing the number of Maori and Pacific Island children to 34 (24 Maori and 10 Pacific Island children).

The research samples

Of the 122 children from Discontinued and Not Discontinued groups who had received Reading Recovery tuition in 1978, 68 were selected for the present study. No exclusions were made on the basis of achievement: the reasons for exclusion were ethnic group membership not clear (five cases), non-availability (six cases), insufficient time in the programme (six cases), absent during testing (one case), majority group excluded by matching (36 cases). There were six samples, shown in Table 9.

TABLE 9	Study samples		
Polynesian		**European***	
Maori			
1 12 with 2 Maori parents		1 E matched to 1 on entry testing	
2 12 with 1 Maori and 1 European parent		2 E matched to 2 on entry testing	
Pacific Island			
3 10 with 2 parents from the same Island group		3 E matched to 3 on entry testing	
Total	34	34	

* European refers to white children from English-speaking homes, also referred to by the Maori term 'Pakeha'.

TABLE 10	Lesson analysis – reading				
Group	Sample	Lessons per week	Books read per lesson	New books per lesson	Books reread (mean accuracy)
Maori	1	1.47	2.50	1.23	94.97
Maori-European	2	1.59	2.07	1.12	94.34
Pacific Island	3	1.52	2.51	1.17	95.08
European	1 E	1.59	2.16	1.21	95.57
European	2 E	1.58	2.15	1.13	95.63
European	3 E	1.96	2.06	1.22	96.47

Results

Lessons per week

Daily lessons are a requirement in the Reading Recovery programme. The present analysis has shown that in the field trials this ideal condition was a long way from realisation. In the six subgroups the average number of lessons per week ranged from 1.47 to 1.96 (Table 10) although five per week were scheduled. Sickness, weekday holidays, absenteeism for other than health reasons and not being able to arrange for the lessons because of other school activities are the probable reasons for the low averages. They are not accounted for by teachers having to relieve in other classes or to take on other responsibilities and the school holidays were excluded from the calculations. There was a much lower rate of instruction than the programme called for, and this points to the need for Reading Recovery teachers to be active in reducing interference with daily lessons.

Average number of lessons for each group

The average number of lessons for each group ranged from 22.50 to 25.33. The lowest time was given to Pacific Island children and the highest time to Maori children. The differences are not important as the variability from child to child within the groups was very great.

Reading

Number of books per lesson

The children read between two and three books per lesson, the range of the six subgroups being 2.06 to 2.51 (Table 10). This implements the recommendations for teaching. It was suggested that the children should begin the lesson by reading one or two easy stories (books) and that later in the lesson a new book would be introduced by the teacher and then tried by the child. At least half of this reading was rereading texts previously read successfully.

New books per lesson

What was the rate at which new books were introduced? The averages ranged from 1.12 to 1.23 books per lesson (Table 10). The teachers exceeded the requirement to try to introduce a new book per lesson. The teacher was skilfully selecting books to suit the particular child's language, concept and reading development which the teacher was acutely aware of, and she was working individually with each child which meant that careful selection was possible. A new book meant a book which had not previously been worked on; it did not necessarily mean a step-up in difficulty level. Sometimes this occurred; at other times the child read at the same level of difficulty. The teachers aimed to move children as rapidly as possible through the various levels of the graded readers while allowing for two other things—quantities of easy reading and the use of many different reading series and story books. The number of new books read is consistent with these aims.

The measure of difficulty of the texts

Running Records of the child's responses (correct responses, errors and self-corrections) taken on the second reading of a new book allowed for a calculation of the accuracy with which a child read a book. Teachers usually took a Running Record before moving the child to another book, to obtain a quantitative check on the quality of the child's reading. The mean accuracy level of the six subgroups ranged from 94.34 to 96.47, implying that the children were managing to read the texts in effective ways.

Stories written

The teaching procedures required the teachers to have a story-writing section in every lesson. The records show that they did not achieve this. The average number of stories written each week ranged from 0.86 to 1.05, never matching the number of lessons for any group (Table 11).

TABLE 11	Lesson analysis – writing			
Group	Sample	Lessons per week	Stories per week	Stories per session
Maori	1	1.47	1.02	0.66
Maori-European	2	1.59	0.86	0.55
Pacific Island	3	1.52	1.00	0.68
European	1 E	1.59	0.99	0.66
European	2 E	1.58	1.05	0.69
European	3 E	1.96	0.96	0.56

The average number of stories per session ranged from 0.55 to 0.69 (Table 11).

Summary of the lesson analyses

There is a similarity across groups in the average number of sessions, the new books per lesson, the books read per lesson, and the mean accuracy levels. There is also similarity in the writing activities. At this level of analysis differences between ethnic groups in the way the programme was implemented were minimal. *Differences between the recommendations for teaching and what occurred were pronounced. The good results achieved were gained on the risky foundation of a partial implementation of the recommended programme.* Reading Recovery teachers should monitor how well they are implementing the programme so that the feedback can alert them to the areas which need closer attention.

On the basis of these data it is not possible to estimate what would happen if the recommended programme of intensive instruction were to be implemented. One might predict faster progress and a shorter intervention period. On the other hand, the shifts demanded of these children were radical compared with classroom progressions. It may be that this present rate is as fast as such children can move. No amount of guessing or argument at this stage will answer this question. Further data from a fully implemented programme would be required.

Undoubtedly, absences from school interfered with full implementation of the programme. This may indicate that, when the programme is introduced, parents need to be consulted and a verbal contract to maximise the opportunity for the child should be entered into by both the home and school.

It may not be realistic to expect the average number of lessons to equal the number of days available for teaching but it is quite possible to make 'Stories Written' equal the number of lessons.

6   THE THREE-YEAR FOLLOW-UP, 1981
Marie M. Clay and Barbara Watson

The research questions

Two questions were raised by educators in relation to long-term outcomes of the Reading Recovery programme.

- Were the children who had Reading Recovery programmes in 1978 continuing to progress with the average groups in their classes in December 1981?
- Was the Reading Recovery programme suitable for Maori children?

The Reading Recovery programme undertook a difficult task. Children with the poorest performance in reading at 6:0 were selected. It was against normal expectations that such children from the low end of the achievement distribution could be brought to average levels of attainment in as little time as 13 to 14 school weeks in both reading and writing. Above-average levels of attainment would not be expected. It would be against normal expectations for many children to retain average placements three years later given the ups and downs of school instruction and of child health and family circumstances. With a partially implemented programme in which children who entered school in Term Three could not receive a full programme because it was only funded for a calendar year, significant results would not be predicted, *yet these Not Discontinued children were included in the three-year follow-up samples.*

The subjects

The ethnic subgroups described in Section 5 were used (see page 75).

Results from earlier studies

Results were extracted from the studies reported in Sections 2 and 3 for these three ethnic groups. Tests of achievement were available for entry to the programme (Initial — **a**); the end of the programme (Discontinuing — **b**); December 1978 (Final — **c**); and December 1979 (Follow-up — **d**). For some children **b** and **c** were the same time (see page 69).

The 'Ready to Read' series of graded readers (plus some graded paragraphs from the Neale analysis [1958]) have been used in several research reports as an ordinal scale of 29 unequal steps used to indicate reading progress (see page 64). The highest level of book read at 90 percent accuracy or above can be used to calculate a mean book level for a group. Table 12 shows similar trends for all subgroups on mean book level with the Maori and Pacific Island groups slightly lower than the Europeans at **a**, **b**, and **c** and increasingly so at **d**.

Schonell R1, a word reading test, was used at the same testing points. Raw scores from this test are given in Table 13. The reader will note:

- the exceedingly low scores of all groups at entry to the programme

- comparable gains but low test scores at the end of the programme (Discontinuing) and at the end of 1978 because this test was unable to capture the magnitude and variety of the changes in reading behaviours that occurred at this level

- more or less equivalent status of the groups in December 1979 when the test provided a more reliable and valid estimate of reading level.

Follow-up after three years

Class placements

The six-year-olds in 1978 were about nine years old by December 1981. They were therefore suitably placed after four years at school in either Standard 2 or 3 under the promotion policies of New Zealand schools. There are three educational reasons why some might be located in Standard 2.

- They had entered school in the second half of 1977 and had three or more years in the Junior classes 1 to 3.

- They entered school early in 1977 and being slower learners or through life circumstances (for example,

TABLE 12	Mean book levels on four occasions					
Group	Sample	N	Entry	Discontinuing	End of 1978	End of 1979
			a	b	c	d
Maori	1	12	4.42	12.42	13.75	19.91
Maori-European	2	12	5.83	14.58	16.42	21.75
Pacific Island	3	10	3.00	11.50	12.50	19.90
European	1 E	12	4.58	14.58	15.92	23.83
European	2 E	12	5.75	14.92	16.92	23.18
European	3 E	10	3.90	13.20	14.20	22.60

TABLE 13	Schonell R1 raw scores on four occasions					
Group	Sample	N	Entry	Discontinuing	End of 1978	End of 1979
			a	b	c	d
Maori	1	12	1.75	6.58	8.50	18.45
Maori-European	2	12	2.08	7.42	10.92	20.00
Pacific Island	3	10	1.00	5.90	8.10	20.10
European	1 E	12	1.17	8.25	9.42	20.83
European	2 E	12	2.75	7.67	10.25	20.27
European	3 E	10	0.70	4.60	7.40	20.50

TABLE 14	Class placements by age at 1 January 1981 (percentages)			
Age	**Group**	**Below S2**	**S2**	**Above S2**
8:0 – 8:11	Total	0	38	5
	Polynesian[1]	0	16	2
	European	0	22	3
Age	**Group**	**Below S3**	**S3**	**Above S3**
9:0 – 9:11	Total	1	24	0
	Polynesian	0	16	0
	European	1	8	0

1 See Table 9 page 75.

TABLE 15	Schonell and Peters achievement ages for the Total group and ethnic subgroups in S2 and S3 (December 1981)					
Group	**N**	**Schonell R1**		**Peters Spelling**	
		M	**SD**	**M**	**SD**
Total	68	9.04	1.36	9.28	1.79
European	34	9.28	1.34	9.31	1.50
Polynesian	34	8.80	1.37	9.25	2.06

TABLE 16	Mean achievement ages of each ethnic subgroup by class (December 1981)				
Class	**Group**	**N**	**Burt (NZ)***	**Schonell R1**	**Peters Spelling**
S2	Maori	10	7:5 – 8:0	8:1	8:5
	European	15	9:1 – 9:6	9:0	8:8
	Pacific Island	6	8:8 – 9:3	9:2	9:1
	European	7	9:5 – 10:0	9:5	9:0
S3	Maori	14	8:8 – 9:3	9:0	9:5
	European	9	10:1 – 10:6	9:7	10:1
	Pacific Island	4	10:5 – 11:0	10:0	11:0
	European	3	11:4 – 11:9	10:9	11:5

* The New Zealand revision of the Burt Test gives score equivalents in age bands.

illness, changes of school, family events) they required three years or more in the Junior classes 1 to 3.

- They were in schools where promotion rates were slower than average because of the entry characteristics of the total population of the school.

Every ex-Reading Recovery child was either in Standard 2 or 3 when this follow-up study was complete. Table 14 reports the number of children at or above class level for age at 1 January 1981 for the Total group and for the subgroups.

It is clear that schools placed the ex-Reading Recovery children according to age for class in almost all cases.

Follow-up test results
Time available between the signing of the contract for this research and the end of the school year determined the selection of tests.

- The Burt Word Reading Vocabulary Test (New Zealand Council for Educational Research 1981) was used because it provided norms for New Zealand children.
- The Schonell Word Reading Vocabulary Test (Schonell R1) was used because it provided a check with earlier Reading Recovery assessments. (Table 13).
- Peters Word Spelling Test (1970) was used to capture control over writing vocabulary.

Text reading could not be assessed because of the time constraints. Tests were administered by a team of five independent trained testers.

These test results allow an evaluation to be made of one of the major claims for the Reading Recovery programme. Children are kept in the programme until they can rejoin an average group in their class and the aim has been to equip them with independent learning strategies that will enable them to maintain that position. Had this been achieved?

Table 15 reports achievement ages for the Total group and two ethnic subgroups in December 1981 when the children were completing Standard 2 or 3. Group means for reading and spelling were at expected levels for class placement. For the purpose of these analyses it has been assumed that a child in Standard 2 with an achievement age of 8:0 to 9:0 years should find the class programme within his ability. The range of Standard 3 was taken as 9:0 to 10:0 years. *This does not take time of year into account.*

Table 16 shows the mean achievement ages according to class placement for each ethnic subgroup. At the end of 1981 children were making the following progress.

- For the European and Pacific Island groups in Standard 2 (N = 28) mean test scores were within the age band for class placement.
- For the European and Pacific Island groups in Standard 3 (N = 16) mean test scores were within the age band for class placement.
- For Maori children in Standard 2 (N = 10) mean reading scores were at or just below the lower limit defined as satisfactory for class level in this study but the mean spelling score was above this limit.

TABLE 17	Raw scores on Burt, Schonell and Peters tests for all subgroups, December 1981 (ages 8:0–9:11)							
Group	**Sample**	**N**	**Burt (NZ)**		**Schonell R1**		**Peters**	
			M	**SD**	**M**	**SD**	**M**	**SD**
Maori	1	12	46.42	17.15	33.67	13.94	28.58	11.12
Maori-European	2	12	48.00	14.24	41.42	13.99	29.27	8.95
Pacific Island	3	10	59.00	16.01	45.40	13.24	33.10	9.40
European	1 E	12	58.17	15.85	43.63	11.37	32.25	5.74
European	2 E	12	57.67	15.66	36.18	13.47	31.58	6.68
European	3 E	10	63.70	15.31	49.20	13.19	33.40	5.48

TABLE 18	Lowest, highest and mean scores for subgroups (ages 8:0 – 9:11)					
	Lowest		**Mean**		**Highest**	
Group	**Maori**	**European**	**Maori**	**European**	**Maori**	**European**
Burt (NZ)	6.1 – 6.6	7.0 – 7.5	8.1 – 8.6	9.1 – 9.6	12.3 – 12.8*	12.3 – 12.8*
Schonell R1	6.3	7.2	8.6	9.3	11.1	12.1
Peters Spelling	6.1	7.1	9.1	9.3	12.4	12.7
Ethnic group	**Pacific Is.**	**European**	**Pacific Is.**	**European**	**Pacific Is.**	**European**
Burt (NZ)	7.1 – 7.6	6.6 – 7.0	9.3 – 9.8	10.0 – 10.5	12.3 –12.8*	12.3 – 12.8*
Schonell R1	7.5	7.5	9.5	9.9	11.6	12.1
Peters Spelling	6.6	7.6	9.9	9.8	12.7	12.3

*   Ceiling level of New Zealand norms on test.

- For Maori children in Standard 3 (N = 14) mean reading scores were at the lower limit defined as satisfactory for class level in this study but the mean spelling score was above this level.

In an analysis which avoided the reading age bands of the Burt test by using raw scores of the Burt, Schonell and Peters tests, Maori groups had scores which were lower than Pacific Island or European children in every instance but the levels of scoring were satisfactory for class levels (Table 17).

Table 18 reports the lowest and highest scores of each subgroup. The ranges of scores were two to three years above and below the means.

7 NATIONAL MONITORING, 1984–1988*

Annual surveys were carried out by the Department of Education from the beginning of the expansion of Reading Recovery (1982–1984) to national coverage in 1988. The feasibility of national implementation of such a strategy is of considerable interest both within and beyond New Zealand.

Reading Recovery went through three years of development and four years of researched trials in various parts of the country (1976–1983) before the Department of Education adopted a policy to slowly expand the programme to give it national coverage. In the 1984 school year the programme reached over 3000 children, and despite a change of Government the expansion policy continued.

Each year, from 1984 to 1988, the Department of Education called for returns on the delivery of the programme in the following way. The central office of the Department approved a data collection form which was distributed through the Liaison Inspector in each Education Board area to Reading Recovery tutors who checked that each school running a programme filed a

return recording the outcome of their year's operation. These forms were analysed by the Department annually as an accountability check on the operation of the programme.

Who needs a Reading Recovery programme?

We know from much recent research that preschool children pay attention to stories and to print and have some ideas about what reading and writing are. This has been called 'emerging literacy', an apt term (Strickland and Morrow, 1989).

In their first year of school, children should have rich opportunities to learn more about literacy in a good classroom programme because most will be able to move successfully into literacy learning in reading and writing. I have described this as a transition period when children translate their previous competencies into ways of responding which work within the demands and opportunities of that classroom programme (Clay, 1991a). Most children's responses to literacy instruction show fluctuation and variance in the first months of school but by the end of the first year it is possible to distinguish those who are having some trouble making the transition and those who are clearly falling behind the large group of children who are succeeding. Some of these children have been sick and absent for long periods, others seem to be confused by the complexities of literacy, and still others take longer to learn. Reading Recovery offers such children supplementary help to make the transition to being effective literacy learners. What they now need is to learn at an accelerated rate to catch up with their classmates.

Many critics have not understood that the teaching procedures used in Reading Recovery are not recommended for the majority of children; they are able to succeed in a variety of classroom programmes. The few children who need Reading Recovery are those who find it hard to develop effective processing for reading, or for writing, in their school's programme. *The aspects of the complex learning that are most troublesome will vary from child to child.* This is one reason why no classroom programme in the first year of instruction will be adequate for all children: those who fail have problem diagnoses which differ one from another. It is also why each teaching programme must be individually designed for each child.

The Reading Recovery programme fits into the first two years of any education system in this way. Children are offered a sound classroom programme in the first year of school and then, if need be, a second chance to make a satisfactory transition once it can be established reliably

* While the data collection and analysis are not something I can take credit for, I appreciate being given permission by the Department of Education to publish this paper and acknowledge the vast amount of work contributed to this report by many teachers, tutors and administrators. This report was first published in the *New Zealand Journal of Educational Studies*, Vol. 25, No. 1, 1990, pp. 61–70. Reprinted with permission.

that such extra help is needed. Results from research studies in three countries (Clay, 1985; Pinnell, DeFord and Lyons, 1988; Wheeler 1986) lead to the conclusion that most children *will* be able to make the transition if they receive the supplementary help offered in Reading Recovery from specially trained teachers in a short-term intervention. The goal is to alter the trajectory of each child's progress, and bring as many low-achieving children as possible up to the average band of performance in their classes with sufficient independence to continue to work at or beyond this level of achievement in reading and writing. Such a goal runs counter to the expectations of many educators but it has been reached by a high proportion of Reading Recovery children.

All prevention programmes are likely to deliver treatments to individuals who may not have needed them. (The immunisation of infants against whooping cough provides one example.) Early intervention programmes involve a prediction about future risk, of sickness in the medical field, or in the present case, of educational failure. Such predictions involve the system in making judgements about how much risk they are prepared to take, and those judgements determine the limits that are placed on the availability of the treatment. (Recent arguments about who should get into Reading Recovery focus on this issue, e.g. Glynn *et al.*, 1989; Nicholson, 1989.)

There are, therefore, two different problems for an education system to solve; first, how to deliver good first instruction in literacy, and second, what kind of supplementary opportunity of an intensive kind to provide for individuals who are low-achieving in that good instruction programme. Beginner instruction cannot be all things to all children, and a second opportunity programme should be available to children with unsatisfactory learning histories in the first year of school.

Organisational issues

The following discussion relates to some aspects of the implementation plan for Reading Recovery.

The programme is an intervention delivered in the 'real world' of schools, by good classroom teachers with special training. The instruction must be varied to meet individual differences and it is delivered during individual lessons for variable periods but always for the shortest necessary period.

A school decides whether to adopt the programme and whether to have one or more experienced junior class teachers trained. Then the programme becomes available to the lowest-achieving children who have been at school

one year not excluding any category of children in normal classrooms for any reason.

This basis of selection overcomes several possible problems.

- It avoids categorising children on the basis of problem diagnoses, because it selects children who are not progressing in achievement in relation to the progress of their classmates.
- It avoids trying to identify which children are at-risk before they have even been given a fair chance to succeed in a good classroom programme.
- It avoids some of the errors that teachers might make if they tried to select children earlier.
- Chances of wrong identification are further reduced because teachers have to select the extreme cases, who are relatively easy to identify, and the criteria of selection are performance in those day-to-day literacy activities which teachers know about.

When resources are in short supply principals have sometimes suggested that children with the greatest need could be excluded from the programme in favour of children whose problems are less extreme and who are more likely to respond to treatment. If this step is taken the programme becomes one aimed at improving performance but not aimed at the prevention of reading and writing difficulties in the education system. It would be a case of selecting children into the programme who were most likely to succeed without it, and excluding from the programme the children least likely to succeed without it. It becomes a programme based on discrimination against a group of children compared with a programme based on equity principles. If teaching time is available, and children with the greatest need have not been excluded, schools may wish to include children whose problems are less extreme. There is no reason why this individual instruction will not be facilitating and helpful to any child, since the instruction is individually designed to meet the pupil's needs.

The percentage of children reached in this strategy to reduce literary failure depends, then, on the resources available. Selection is made from the poorest achievers, and an education system might reach 5, 10 or even 20 percent of children in the age group. Some schools in affluent districts in the USA have decided to help the lowest 30 percent of their children. It must be remembered that there is a spin-off effect from having a Reading Recovery programme in the school. When the classroom teacher knows that her two or three lowest achievers are working individually with the Reading Recovery teacher she has more time to give to the lower achievers in her class who will not be getting individual help.

The prevention strategy already operates in very different education systems, following on from very different first-year instruction programmes. It allows for the assumption that different causative factors will be operating for different individuals. It addresses the need to provide different sequences of instruction to meet individual needs and for those programmes to vary in length, short for some and up to 20 weeks for others. It respects the fact that school and education systems are of very different sizes and types, and that their intake populations differ. As a general preventive strategy it seems to have been able to be adapted to most settings, although the problems of remoteness and very small schools present the most difficulties.

Children entering the programme reach criteria for being discontinued in 12 to 20 weeks of daily, 30-minute lessons, individually designed and individually delivered. The criteria require those discontinued from the programme to have become independent learners within the average band of the classroom to which they belong and to be able to survive in that classroom 'with a not-noticing teacher'—the most risky scenario. High success rates obtained in a short time are needed to make the programme cost-effective and a high-quality programme based on sound training of the teachers is required to achieve these outcomes.

The cut-off time of 20 weeks is arbitrary but is part of the planning to make the prevention programme cost-effective, for otherwise it would be in danger of accumulating a clientele who need long-term help. Then help would not be available to the continuing flow of low-achieving children finishing their first year at school, who need short-term help. Again, a school or system with ample resources could set the upper limit of time in the programme at some other level but it is likely that the few children who have not accelerated in their progress within that period need a different kind of help and should in any case be referred for a specialist report and special needs programming after about 20 weeks in Reading Recovery.

So the actual percentages of all school children helped by such an early intervention strategy as Reading Recovery will depend on the resources an education system is prepared to allocate, the quality of staff training, the effectiveness with which the programme is implemented, and the success of professionals in explaining the benefits of the early intervention strategy for the learners and for the education system (Clay, 1987).

The programme currently operates nationally in New Zealand, in parts of Australia, in the state of Ohio, and other parts of the USA (Clay, 1987), and in England. As education systems differ, differences in the management of the programme have been necessary affecting age of entry, time spent in the programme, criteria for entry and for discontinuing.

Five years of operation in New Zealand

Table 19 (page 84) presents figures for the following:

- children in the birth cohort (Column 1)
- children admitted to the programme (Column 2)
- children discontinued within 20 weeks at average band levels for their classroom; full programme (Column 3)
- children entering the programme late in the school year, having incomplete programmes of under 20 weeks who will continue in the following year (Column 4)   (Section 8, page 86.)
- children leaving the school (Column 5)
- children referred for special reports and special needs programmes (Column 6).   (Section 8, page 86.)

In the second part of the table these are expressed as percentages of the birth cohort.

1   Changes between 1984 and 1988 are consistent with the policy of expansion of the programme, and its infrastructure (for training and support), to an increasing percentage of low-achieving children (Column 2).

2   About two-thirds of the annual intake are discontinued during the calendar year in New Zealand and in each country where it has been tried. Because children spend variable time in the programme, no longer than necessary, and because each teaching place in the programme allows for about two-and-a-half children to enter per calendar year, about one-third of the children receive an incomplete programme (Columns 3 and 4). (The reason these children are 'not discontinued' is that they have only been in the programme a few weeks and have not yet reached discontinuing criteria for independent processing and a high chance of survival back in the classroom.) So in each calendar year one-third of the children must be expected to enter the programme late in the year and continue in the programme in the following year. The actual number of children carried over from the previous year was only recorded in the national returns in this form in 1987 and 1988.

3   The percentage of children leaving the school (Column 5) occurs through mobility of families, and

TABLE 19	Status of children leaving Reading Recovery over five years in New Zealand: numbers and percentages					
Year	Birth cohort N 1	In R–R N 2	Full R–R N 3	Incomplete N 4	Left R–R N 5	Refer on N 6
1984	49574	3200	2036	867	176	128
1985	51211*	5323	3093	1615	357	238
1986	49044	7468	4536	2097	475	360
1987	49789	9240	5904	2509	512	313
1988	49482	10511	6494	2976	648	390
	%	%	%	%	%	%
1984	100	6.45	4.11	1.75	0.35	0.26
1985	100	10.39	6.04	3.15	0.70	0.46
1986	100	15.23	9.25	4.27	0.96	0.73
1987	100	18.56	11.86	5.04	1.03	0.63
1988	100	21.24	13.12	6.01	1.31	0.80

*   1984 six-year-old population.
Figures in the top half of Table 19 are those given in the End of Year Summary Tables of the Department of Education.

TABLE 20	Children referred for further help as a percentage of the district birth cohort*								
	1	2	3	4	5	6	7	8	9	10
1984	0.21	0.27	0.59	0.27	0.57	0.68	0.03	0.91	0.80	0.77
1985	0.44	0.32	0.33	0.32	0.08	0.52	0.30	0.44	0.54	0.51
1986	1.03	0.78	1.09	0.71	0.91	0.11	1.20	0.47	0.76	0.55
1987	0.74	0.76	0.95	0.55	0.57	0.23	1.45	0.47	0.53	0.43
1988	0.99	0.95	0.75	1.09	0.83	0.36	0.60	0.57	0.72	0.40

*   Derived from the End of Year Summary Tables of the Department of Education: 50 returns from 10 New Zealand education boards, 1984–1988.

while every effort is made to include them in a Reading Recovery programme in their new schools, there are no data on this group.

4   Column 6 reports the low percentages of children judged by the school team not to meet the discontinuing criteria of Reading Recovery, not predicted to succeed within the average band in their classrooms in both reading and writing with a 'not-noticing teacher' and referred for a specialist report and recommendations for programming for a longer period.

The figures in Table 20 are confirmatory, showing that the same levels of results were being obtained in each of 10 Education Board districts. These figures are not proportions: they are percentages, showing that very rarely has the percentage of children referred to specialists reached the one percent level.

It was predicted that the number of children referred for specialist reports would rise because of the increasing willingness of schools to refer children as early as six-and-a-half and the psychological services recognising the importance of their role in making this early intervention strategy work. There is still a residual reluctance in schools to refer children and in the psychological services to see such children at six-and-a-half years, despite the availability of detailed records of their response to individual efforts to teach them over a 20-week period. This may result from optimistic hope that things will come right, or priority rating on urgent cases in waiting lists. If such reluctance were overcome, and preventive action given more weight, one would expect the percentage of children referred for specialist reports to continue to increase, towards and above one percent.

There is a less positive reason why these percentages might increase. Reading Recovery is a programme which calls for high effort: the changes in children who are struggling are hard-won, so continued quality of programme implementation is needed to keep the percentage of children who need to be referred for further help as low as possible. If the quality of the programme should drop, if teachers expect the changes to occur without the immense effort that has been invested by teachers to this point, the success of a prevention programme and its acceptability could result in lowered effort or quality and fewer children would be discontinued.

National implementation has been possible

The figures in Table 19 indicate that the programme has sustained its promise of providing a second chance to learn literacy for many children while at the same time expanding to national coverage. To date, the training and organisational support arrangements have maintained its quality as indicated by the operational figures. A small national coordination team, and local tutors training teachers and managing the local district running of the programme have proved to be effective support for the expansion. The teacher training is an inservice programme, with the Reading Recovery trainees working as 'apprentices' under tuition and supervision during their first year of operation. To allow for expansion and replacement of staff who leave for various reasons it has been necessary to train a group of tutors every two years as the programme has expanded.

Current issues

The quality of the data

These results report only the functioning of the children at the time of discontinuing from Reading Recovery or at the end of the school year, or at referral for specialist reports. And they are careful but 'in-house' assessments by the teachers delivering the programme, rather than the result of independent surveys. Two research studies have shown that three years later most children retain their gains and continue to function within the average band of their classes (Clay and Watson, 1982; Pinnell et al., 1988).

Participation of schools

Expansion of the programme depends, in part, upon the willingness of schools to opt into the programme and to find resources to mount it and expand it in their schools. Participation increased from 409 to 1107 schools in 1988. One might conclude that schools place value on having these children helped to make the transition into literacy and work within the average band of their classrooms.

Reading Recovery under 'Tomorrow's Schools'*

In many ways this programme was ahead of the administrative reforms in New Zealand. Ideally the decision to mount a Reading Recovery programme should be made by an individual school, after considering that school's needs. The goal of having an early intervention programme was to improve literacy learning within that school and reduce strains on the upper-primary classes by having fewer literacy problems in the upper-primary school. A team of teachers, often the principal, the senior teacher in the junior school, and the selected Reading Recovery teachers make the decisions about how many children and teachers they need to meet their particular goals. The national constraints have been in the advice to make the programme efficient and effective by selecting the poorest achievers not excepting anyone, and setting the 20-week limit for time in the programme. (Even that is flexible because if the school has the resources they are free to take in children for longer periods. They may also admit mainstreamed children with special needs reports, as long as they are not excluding children for whom the programme was designed. This means providing for extra teaching time.) Decisions about the programme within a school should be made by the school's team in the interests of the needs of that school. That fits well with the 'Tomorrow's Schools' model.

Criticism of the entry criteria

A critique of the programme's research (Nicholson, 1989) and the Reading Recovery in Context report (Glynn et al., 1989) claim that children may be entering the programme for whom it is unnecessary. I accept that this is inherent in a prevention strategy. The Reading Recovery in Context report recommends a conservative approach to such a risk in the form of fixed criteria for entry, set low and based only on text reading level. This issue deserves a detailed response that does not belong here but schools should bear three arguments in mind.

- Establishing a cut-off limit for entry to the programme in terms of text reading alone (compared with the six evaluation measures available) increases the possibility of selection errors and increases the risk of the prevention strategy incurring high failure rates.
- A conservative cut-off point for entry into a prevention programme increases the risk that there will be children not included in the programme who subsequently

---

* Major administration reforms shifted schools from district control to local school management by October, 1989.

fail. Such selection errors reduce the chances of the programme being seen as viable and therefore being funded. Making too many selection errors will threaten the survival of a programme.

- A child may be able to read text tolerably well and may not be developing writing vocabulary. In the profile of measurements used with Reading Recovery children this is regarded as an indication of help needed. The Reading Recovery in Context research paid no attention to the writing side of literacy.

Overview of the achievements

The spread to near-national coverage and the results of Reading Recovery in numbers of children discontinued show that this is a programme which schools and teachers have been able to mount and deliver. They have seen a high proportion of the children who have immense difficulty making the transition into formal literacy brought to a fair measure of independence in classroom work in a relatively short period of time. The results challenge much accumulated wisdom about literacy problems; clearly they are alterable variables for many children.*

Although the percentage of children who need longer-term help is low they are a group about which we need more information. The Research Division of the New Zealand Ministry of Education funded a research project directed to this problem.

| 8 THE READING RECOVERY SUBGROUPS STUDY, 1991 |
| Bryan Tuck and Marie M.Clay |

As people become familiar with the Reading Recovery programme and notice the consistency with which it can bring high numbers of children to average band performance in their classrooms, the next questions to be asked are about the unsuccessful subgroup, the children who do not meet this criterion. Questioners are concerned about the policy in Reading Recovery that these children be referred for a specialist report around the twentieth week of the programme, and what happens to these children after they leave Reading Recovery. The erroneous

---

* The Research and Statistics Division of the Ministry of Education, Wellington, has published summaries of Reading Recovery data for 1989, 1990, 1991 and 1992. Latest figures show that the programme is reaching 24% of children and more rural schools have been involved.

---

assumption is often made that these children have failed to make progress on the programme; that is not so. Although they have failed to achieve the average level for their classes they may be making steady but slow progress.

This report deals with information on three Reading Recovery subgroups, and one of those subgroups consisted of children who were referred out of the programme for a specialist report. The study confirms the current implementation practices but suggests implications for fine-tuning the delivery of further services to children who cannot be successfully discontinued in a Reading Recovery intervention. The results of this research have implications for the policies and provisions of the Ministry of Education and the practices of schools.

The research design

The samples

An analysis was made of detailed records kept by Reading Recovery teachers for three groups of children (N = 420) taught in New Zealand in 1988. The analysis compared change over time in the achievements of children who reached average-band performance for their classes, with children who did not reach this criterion level, and required specialist reports. Also studied were a group of children who entered the programme late in the school year and whose programmes were continued after the long summer vacation.

Random samples were drawn from national returns of **a**) all children in Reading Recovery in December 1988 who had successfully completed their programmes (i.e. they were Discontinued), and **b**) all children who entered late in 1988 and whose programmes were to be completed in 1989 (i.e. To Be Continued). We called for complete lesson and programme records for 988 Discontinued children, and 906 To Be Continued children.

Every child who was unable to successfully complete the programme (390 children out of a total of 9860) made up the third research group. They were called the Referred group because the appropriate next move for these children was that they should be referred for a specialist report.

Teachers returned the records as requested but *full* records were available only for a proportion of the randomly selected children. From those children with full records we selected all the Referred children (140) and matched them with Discontinued (140) and To Be Continued children (140) to form triplet sets, controlling for school and teacher difference. Other approaches to

TABLE 21	Details of sampling						
Group A	In Reading Recovery 1988	Records requested	Records returned	Full records returned	Final sample	Final as % (of column 1)	Sampling ratios
Referred	390	380	272	140	140	35.9	1: 2.76
To Be Continued	2976	906	832	648	140	4.7	1:21.35
Discontinued	6494	988	942	577	140	2.2	1:46.36

sampling would have produced an impossibly small Referred group since it is known to be about 1 percent of the age cohort (Clay, 1990) and the main thrust of this project was to investigate child outcomes and policy implications for this group.

However, because of these sampling procedures generalisation from these samples to the total population of children who enter Reading Recovery must be tentative. There was one Referred child in the research sample for every three such children in the national programme; there was one To Be Continued child in the sample for 21 such children in the national programme, and there was one Discontinued child in the sample for 46 such children in the national programme. Table 21 sets out sampling details.

Measurement and progress
Seven tests were routinely administered at entry to the programme and at exit (called Discontinuing). Six were from the Diagnostic Survey (Clay, 1985) and one was the nationally standardised Burt Oral Word Reading Test (New Zealand Council for Education Research, 1981).

Interpretations of the research results should acknowledge that while these tests all capture important changes over time in literacy learning they fall into two distinct groups, according to whether the learning occurs in a rela-

tively open-ended variable like text reading level or in a finite set of information like all the letters of the alphabet. Finite sets of learning show what is called 'ceiling effects' on the tests as all learners move towards knowledge of the entire set of learning, and this places limitations on quantitative analyses of the data.

Once a week teachers plotted for their own information the highest level of book on a gradient of text difficulty read at or above 90 percent accuracy, producing a graph of reading progress. While this appears to be linear in shape for most children it is important to note that as the child becomes able to read more difficult texts he is reading more words, in longer stories, written in more complex language. The steps in book level are unequal: those higher on the scale involve bigger increases in the amount to be read and new types of challenges.

Teachers also kept a cumulative record of writing vocabulary used during lessons, including in the count each new word the child demonstrated that he could write correctly without assistance. (Correctness is used to achieve valid scoring by different scorers; it is acknowledged that children move towards correctness through approximations and partially correct transitions.) Not all teachers kept these records, and those who did, did not necessarily keep records at regular intervals. Therefore not all the records were usable, but most were, even when

TABLE 22	Classification of assessments by ceiling effects
With ceiling effects	**Without ceiling effects**
Letter Identification Finite set of learning	**Text Reading Level** Discontinuing levels halfway up the scale
Dictation (grapho-phonemic scoring) Limited set of learning	**Writing Vocabulary** Ten-minute limit, open-ended
Concepts About Print Limited set of learning	**Burt Oral Word Reading** (NZCER, 1981) Ceiling at 12- to13-year level
Clay Word Test Short list of highest frequency words	

there were missing data points.

Referred children's achievement at follow-up in 1990 was assessed with

- Text Reading of Graded Paragraphs (New Zealand Department of Education, 1984)
- Burt Oral Word Reading (NZCER, 1981)
- Spelling Test (Peters, 1970).

Results

Part One: Progress within the programme

The theory which supports Reading Recovery was derived from studies of children in classrooms learning to read successfully. The intervention conceptualises literacy learning as complex learning, not controlled by any single variable or type of response, but requiring the orchestration of various responses to derive meaning from text. Each of the assessment tasks measures different clusters of responses all of which are necessary but none of which is sufficient on its own to 'cause' success in literacy learning.

A large proportion of children in Reading Recovery have entry scores close to zero and it was uncertain how well the Reading Recovery assessment instruments would discriminate between the subgroups at entry, during the programme, and at final testing. It was of interest to know whether at entry those children who would be discontinued could be distinguished from those who would be referred.

Each assessment in the set used to select children for the programme, monitor their progress, and make decisions about referral or discontinuing worked better than one would expect with such low-scoring children (Clay and Tuck, 1991) but the findings did not suggest that assessment be limited to any single measure or a reduced set of measures. The use of only text reading, or text reading and writing vocabulary is not recommended as each of the seven assessments can be related through theory with the progress.

Relationships were found between levels at entry and the probability of being either discontinued or referred. In general the probability of being discontinued is lowest for the group of children with relatively poor levels of performance at entry. However it is also the case that individual children unable to score on some of the entry measures were in the Discontinued group, i.e. they reached a level of skill deemed to be average for their class. There are also examples of children who although ultimately in the Referred group scored relatively well on some of the entrance tests. It was concluded that it would be imprudent to exclude individual children on the basis of entry scores. The graphs of progress in reading and writing for one set of research triplets (Figure 6) clearly demonstrate the variability among individual children. Series A in these graphs plots the progress of a Discontinued child; Series C plots the progress of a Referred child and Series F plots the progress of a child who entered the programme late in the year and was to be continued in the following school year.

FIGURE 6   **Graphs of progress in reading and writing for one set of research triplets**

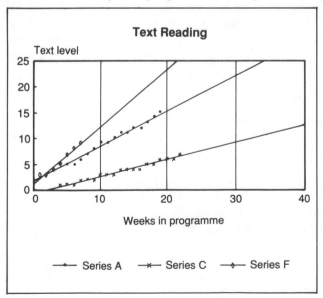

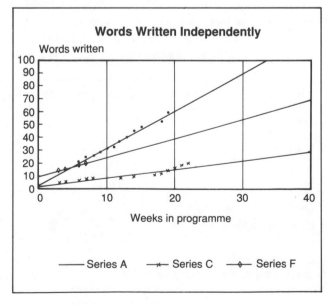

| | Length of time in weeks to | |
Variables	Discontinued	Referred
Text Level	−.53 **	−.11
Letter Identification	−.52 **	−.12
Concepts About Print	−.34 **	−.09
Word Test	−.55 **	−.04
Burt Reading (NZCER, 1981)	−.60 **	−.10
Writing Vocabulary	−.62 **	−.26 **
Dictation	−.61 **	−.23 **

TABLE 23   Correlations between length of time to discontinuing or referral and assessments at entry

** p < 0.01 (one-tailed)

Note: The N for the correlations ranged from 137 to 140.

Correlations between entry scores and length of time in the programme (see Table 23) for the successful children (Discontinued) showed that children with the lowest scores tended to take longer to meet the criteria for discontinuing. They had more to learn. For the Referred children the length of time they spent in the programme tended to be unrelated to performance level at entry.

Both in New Zealand and overseas the average time in the programme ranges from 12 to 15 weeks, and a recommended upper limit has been set at about 20 weeks, at which time children who cannot be discontinued should be referred for a specialist report. While awaiting a specialist recommendation, and when teacher time was available, schools often kept children in Reading Recovery until a decision on further appropriate programming had been made. This study presents no evidence to suggest a change in this practice. However a school must be cautious when deciding to retain children in a Reading Recovery programme for longer than 20 weeks because this decision could limit the opportunity for entry of younger children who need it.

Both Discontinued and Referred groups made important gains in test scores over the period of the intervention. The majority of the Discontinued children were performing at or above the New Zealand national average level of Stanine 5 at exit from the programme on each assessment. Many Referred children also reached these levels on some of the measures. There was overlap between the Discontinued and Referred groups on each of the separate measures. Examples of such distributions of individuals in the two groups for Reading Text levels and Writing Vocabulary are shown in Tables 24 a – d.

As the theory behind the Reading Recovery programme assumes that successful readers and writers learn to bring together information and/or responses from different areas as they problem-solve texts, it is not inconsistent with that theory that Referred children can score relatively well in some areas but still not meet the criteria for discontinuing. Those criteria require that children work relatively independently at problem-solving in all aspects of literacy tasks while reading or writing continuous texts.

A series of checks on data patterns found that the tenth week was the earliest that reliable predictions could be made of whether a child would be discontinued. At this time predictions were successful for between 70 and 85 percent of the cases. *However, this means that from 15 to 30 percent of judgements about outcome would be wrong if made at this time.* An intervention programme affecting children cannot risk such a high level of error. The predictions at 10 weeks were better for Discontinued than for Referred children. Some children with relatively poor levels at 10 weeks make accelerated progress after that time. Because of the high number of incorrect predictions it would be extremely unwise to withdraw children at the tenth week. Only in exceptional individual cases would decisions to refer children earlier for a specialist report be appropriate (see Figure 7, Series C).

TABLE 24a Instructional text level at entry compared with exit level for Discontinued group (N = 140)

Text Level at entry	Level when Discontinued							
	9–10	11–12	13–14	15–16	17–18	19–20	21–22	23+
0	1		1	9	6	1		
1 – 2			5	15	8	4	2	
3 – 4			4	15	12	8		
5 – 6			1	4	7	4	3	1
7 – 8			1	3	2	1	4	
9 – 10				3	2	3		
11 – 12					2	3	2	1
13 – 14					2			

TABLE 24b Instructional text level at entry compared with exit level at referral for Referred group (N = 140)

Text Level at entry	Level when Referred									
	0	1 – 2	3 – 4	5 – 6	7 – 8	9 –10	11–12	13 –14	15 –16	17 –18
0		3	14	10	8	5	7	5	3	
1– 2		3	4	10	11	12	8	3	4	1
3 – 4			3		3	5	8	5	2	
5 – 6							1		1	
7 – 8										
9 –10							1			

TABLE 24c Writing Vocabulary Stanines at entry compared with Stanines at discontinuing for Discontinued group (N=139)

Stanine at entry	Stanine when Discontinued								
	1	2	3	4	5	6	7	8	9
1		3	12	23	33	24	12	1	
2			1	1	7	2	1		1
3			1	2	5	3	2		
4					3	2			

Table 24d Writing Vocabulary Stanines at entry compared with Stanines at referral for Referred group (N = 117)

Stanine at entry	Stanine when Referred								
	1	2	3	4	5	6	7	8	9
1	33	24	30	16	7	3			
2		1	1	1					
3					1				

TABLE 25	Prediction of programme outcomes at 10 weeks: success or failure of the prediction					
	The prediction was a...	Reading	%	Writing	%
All Discontinued and Referred	Success Failure	205 57	78.2[a] 21.8	188 62	75.2[a] 24.8
Discontinued (N = 139)	Success Failure	115 20	85.2 14.8	107 27	79.9 20.1
Referred (N = 139)	Success Failure	90 37	70.9 29.1	81 35	69.8 30.2
No data Discontinued Referred		4 12		5 23	

a Predictions made at 10 weeks as to whether a child would be Discontinued or Referred out of the programme would be successful for about three in four cases in either Reading or Writing. Criteria for prediction: Text Level 5 at week 10 and 20 words written at week 10.

Reading. If the criterion were lowered to Text Level 4 and below (instead of Text Level 5) then there would only be six prediction failures for the Discontinued group, and an increase for the Referred group. If the criterion were raised to Text Level 6 or above there would still be almost as many failures (34) in predictions for the Referred group. If the criterion were raised to Text Level 7 or above there would still be 24 failures. This is accounted for by inspection of the graphs and the fact that those Referred children who make a late run at accelerated progress move through many Reading Book levels in the latter part of their programmes.

Writing. If the criterion were lowered to 17 words or below (instead of 20 words and below) then there would still be 17 prediction failures for the Discontinued group. If the criterion were raised to 23 words or below there would still be 24 failures in the Referred group.

FIGURE 7: **An earlier decision could have been made to refer the child in Series C, certainly by 20 weeks and perhaps earlier than that.**

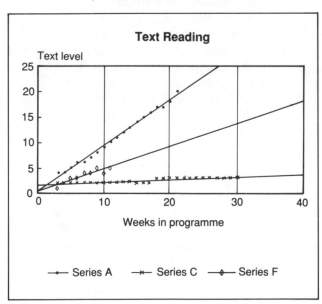

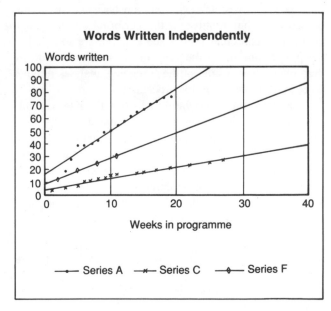

Can children with somewhat higher entry scores be excluded from the programme?

It has been suggested that children who already read texts at Level 7 or above might not need the programme (Glynn *et al.*, 1989). That recommendation assumes that text level is on its own a reliable predictor. Our information shows that individual children can have relatively uneven performance across the various assessments and that it is unwise to rely on only one assessment.

If we accept the risk of predicting only from the text reading assessment, the study leads to the following best prediction.

'If the text level is Level 5 or above after 10 weeks in the programme the probability is high that the child will be discontinued.'

However, this rule failed to correctly predict the outcomes for 22 percent of the combined Discontinued and Referred group. The rule was 'cross-validated' on an independent sample and a similar pattern of 'hits and misses' was observed (Clay. and Tuck, 1991). Prediction failure is thus high at 10 weeks of instruction. Applying some Book Level cutting point around the time children enter the programme would probably produce higher risk of being wrong than we obtained at 10 weeks.

To enter the Reading Recovery programme children must be the lowest achievers in their ordinary classroom. Selection is thus relative to the performance of the age cohort in a particular school and children are admitted to the programme up to the limit of resources set aside by that school. The results of the foregoing analyses provide no reason for changing this procedure.

One interesting observation was that the rates of children whose programmes were interrupted by the long summer holiday were similar to those of children whose total programme fell within one school year in **a**) discontinuing rates and **b**) referral rates. However, a small number of the To Be Continued group were not in Reading Recovery in the following year. The research identified three reasons for not completing their programmes.

- *Change of school.* Children moved schools and were not identified in their new schools.
- *Continued improvement.* Children retested by the Reading Recovery teacher after the summer vacation were then found to be within the average band for their new classes.
- *No teacher resource.* When a Reading Recovery teacher moved to a new school the new Reading Recovery teacher in training would not be able to work

with more than two children who were already half-way through their programmes.

It must be recognised that there is a clear risk of 'slippage' occurring around the long summer vacation.

Part Two: What happens to the 'referrable' children?

A national questionnaire survey was completed, and, with the assistance of a network of Reading Recovery tutors across the country, returns were available for 139 of the 140 Referred children (see Table 26). Of the 45 Referred children in the sample who lived in the Auckland area 44 were located and two educational psychologists interviewed teachers about progress, placements, and instructional assistance in 1989 and 1990, and the children's achievements in reading and spelling were assessed.

Eighty-two percent of referrable children were referred by schools for specialist reports (Table 26). Most were being referred by six-and-a-half years, and this shows an important change from past practice. The study shows that early identification of children who need special help of a continuing kind is possible. Action should be taken to prevent the problem worsening and transfer from Reading Recovery to further specialist teaching on a continuing basis without a break would maximise the carry-over and minimise loss of what has been already learned. This referral rate should be lifted closer to 100 percent.

From the questionnaire returns for the 139 children there were 182 individual service entries. Such services fell into the categories discussed below (Table 27).

Referred children placed in Special Class or mainstreamed with or without an individual educational programme written by a psychologist accounted for 28 percent of the entries. This provides an estimate of the number of children whose literacy learning may be expected to continue to improve but at slow rates.

Resource Teachers of Reading (RTR), and Reading Assistance teachers (RA) might be expected to see, teach, advise and guide the progress of the majority of Referred children not in the foregoing group. This is not the case. Only 24 percent of the entries on the questionnaires showed RTRs and RAs involved in any way. Those entries include placing the child on a waiting list, or offering advice on programming but not teaching the child.

Often the RTR had a pattern of involvement with Referred children which involved three stages. **1**) A Referred child was given individual tutoring for several months until a measure of independence in reading and writing was achieved and then **2**) the RTR provided guid-

TABLE 26	Action taken to refer to a specialist the children who did not reach criteria for discontinuing				
District	**Not applicable or no data**	**Not Referred**	**Psychological Service**	**Direct to RTR** (Resource Teacher of Reading)	**Other**
All districts (N=139)	7	18	82	28	4
Auckland	3	7	28	15	2
Hamilton	2	2	23	2	0
Gisborne	–	3	2	1	1
Napier	–	–	–	1	–
Taranaki	–	–	3	1	–
Wanganui	–	5	6	1	1
Wellington	1	–	3	1	–
Nelson	–	–	3	3	–
Canterbury	–	–	9	2	–
Otago/Southland	1	1	5	1	–
	18%		82%		

TABLE 27	Following referral, action taken to provide services					
District	**Special class**	**Mainstreamed, with or without IEP*, or special needs funds**	**RTR including waiting list**	**Reading help of some kind**	**Other**	**No data No referral No action**
All districts (N=182)	22	29	43	67	21	16
Auckland	8	5	22	29	8	7
Hamilton	4	8	3	17	7	2
Gisborne	1	1	5	5	–	1
Napier	–	1	1	1		–
Taranaki	2	1	1	1	1	–
Wanganui	2	5	1	2		3
Wellington	1	2	1	2		1
Nelson	1	1	3	4	–	–
Canterbury	1	3	5	2	4	1
Otago/Southland	2	2	1	4	1	1
% of entries	28%		23%	36%	11.5%	8%

Note: Table includes multiple entries for some children: 182 entries for 139 children.   * Individual Education Programme.

ance to the classroom teacher and monitored the child's further needs until 3) the support service was provided entirely by the school. Shifts of this kind are appropriate to provide the most facilitating environment for the child in a cost-effective way but this report does not provide data on what criteria were used to guide these shifts and what the implications were for the subsequent progress of the children helped by the RTR.

Reading help delivered by other persons of varied training accounted for 37 percent of the action taken (including placing the child in a small reading group; using an itinerant reading teacher, a teacher aide, a parent helper, a peer tutor or senior student, an ethnic language teacher, a special needs teacher, or in one entry only, a Speld teacher). The time available for the service varied greatly from half an hour a week to daily help, as did the duration of the help, for a month or so to one, two or three terms of the school year.

The student outcome data for the 45 Auckland Referred children who were followed-up and tested for current achievement levels in literacy two years and some months after their Reading Recovery programme ended has some positive features (seven children were functioning within average-band levels for their class, and most special education students could read and write simple texts) but for the remainder the picture is somewhat negative. Too many of the Referred group were working more than a year below their age group, despite the various services delivered to them in the two years following Reading Recovery. (See Clay and Tuck, 1991.)

Two general comments on this further programming can be made:

Multiple concurrent services It is appropriate for Referred children to have help from various services, but preferable that they have the skilled attention of highly trained professionals with sound knowledge of literacy learning. What is particularly problematic is that children with literacy learning difficulties need a consistent approach to their slow build-up of competencies. Different approaches delivered over the same period of time are certain to compound their problems.

Multiple services over time There are likely to be some changes over time as specialists, teachers and parents try to establish the most facilitating programme for an individual child. However, the need for changes should be minimised, by seeking specialist guidance early, and establishing a programme of long-term help rather than spurts of casual short-term help.

While the quantity of 'reading help' available beyond Reading Recovery appears, on the surface, to be satisfactory, the quality and consistency of that instruction for this hard-to-teach group (who make up less than 1 percent of the age group) can be questioned.

A recommendation was made to the Ministry of Education that improvement of this situation be given a high policy priority. Factors requiring attention were identified as follows:

1 Factors relating to more effective delivery of the services, such as

- access to individual specialist teaching for all Referred children not receiving special services
- an initial training for Resource Teachers of Reading prior to appointment with continuing inservice updates
- more Resource Teachers of Reading or Reading Assistance teachers achieving wider coverage throughout the country
- longer periods of service delivery, and closer supervision during the time when schools are being guided by the RTR to provide a continuing programme
- research documentation of the RTR service delivery over three years either nationally, or in selected areas.

2 Factors related to the knowledge barrier about what are effective ways to work with these children. A research and development programme is needed to uncover new and diverse ways to work with this extremely hard-to-teach group, devising both teaching and monitoring procedures for a small group of children who are far from homogeneous in their learning characteristics.

Summary of the study of Reading Recovery subgroups

This study refers to the progress of Reading Recovery children in New Zealand who were taught in 1988, and it examines in detail three subgroups: those who were successful in meeting the criteria of average-band performance for their classrooms, those who had incomplete programmes, and those who should have been referred for specialist reports because of unsuccessful progress. Most children are successful in meeting the programme criteria for discontinuing; only 0.5 to 1 percent of the age cohort fall into the referrable group.

Study of the three subgroups confirms earlier reports about progress during Reading Recovery but provides illustrations of individual variation in **a**) test score patterns, **b**) progress made during the programme, and **c**) the congruence or otherwise of progress when reading is compared with writing.

Although the study found relationships between the entry characteristics of the children and progress in the programme it cautioned against using this information in a deterministic fashion. Predictions of outcome status for individual children from either high or low entry scores, or even after 10 weeks of instruction are likely to be wrong in a significant number of cases. A full programme of instruction (varying according to individual needs from 12 to 20 weeks) provides at present the best practical estimate of which children will need further individual assistance.

For several quite different reasons programmes were not always completed for the group To Be Continued in the following school year. Special effort should be made to allow this group to complete a full Reading Recovery programme. Only 82 percent of referrable children were referred for specialist reports. As such referrals allow for a second opinion on children who are very hard to teach, and provide the means of getting expert advice on further instructional programming, it would be desirable for this to occur for all such children.

While schools have seen the need for the referred children to get individual instruction and have in many cases arranged for this, it does not seem reasonable for such children to be faced with multiple approaches to their problems from different tutors concurrently, or over several years of schooling. Consistency in long-term programming is desirable.

SUMMARY

The challenges

Daily, individual instruction might be expected to produce important shifts in children's reading performance. The Reading Recovery programme was associated with such shifts in all the subgroups studied.

Readers are asked to consider again the degree of challenge accepted by the Reading Recovery programme in the Field Trial year.

---

1 The children with the poorest performance of all the children in their schools at 6 : 0 were selected for instruction. Teachers used no procedures for excluding any children. They dealt with children in the tail of the achievement distribution for the age-group and included:

- bicultural Maori children
- bilingual Pacific Island children
- children with handicaps
- children awaiting Special Class placements.

2 It was against normal expectations that any children in the tail end of the achievement distribution could be brought to average levels of attainment:

- in as little time as 13 to 14 weeks
- in both reading and writing.

Above-average levels of attainment would not be expected.

3 Whatever the levels of attainment at the end of individual tutoring it would be against normal expectations for many children to retain average placements three years later given the ups and downs of school instruction and of child health and family circumstance.

4 It would be almost unreasonable to expect to get any shifts and maintenance of the kinds described with a partially implemented programme which means:

- children who entered school in Term III of the field trial year could not receive a full programme as it was only funded for the calendar year, and
- teachers in the field trial year were subsequently found to be not operating the programme as prescribed.

The gains to 1992

The Reading Recovery programme is an effective programme for reducing the number of children with reading difficulties in New Zealand schools (Clay, 1979; Clay and Watson, 1982). It is a second-chance, early intervention programme. Its aim is to pick up the children who have not begun to read and write after one year at school and provide them with intensive instruction daily and individually. As a result of accelerated progress the children typically leave the programme with average levels of performance in three to six months. The success gained with the poorest performers of the age group at six years runs counter to the assumptions, expectations and experience in most Western education systems. It is probably related to the specific nature of the instruction delivered by well trained teachers (Clay, 1982).

Since 1978 the programme has been developed and gradually expanded. Although it was only partially implemented in New Zealand until about 1988 it won support from teachers, principals, school committees, the Department of Education, the media and the public. Reports of its research and development phase, and of two follow-up studies (one and three years later) support its effectiveness across ethnic groups, and the national monitoring figures show how the programme has spread across the education system to reach around 20 percent of the children.

Quality assurance

The gains were achieved by experienced but non-specialist primary teachers without academic training but who knew how to teach children of this age group, and how, in particular, to teach reading. They were guided by very well trained tutors who fully understood why each of the procedures and requirements were in the programme. The Ministry of Education has ensured that the expansion of the programme only proceeds when this necessary support system is already in place. They have also ensured that clear communications to the rest of the education system preceded each expansion of the programme so that all understood the preventive thrust of the programme.

Training for teachers consists of only 50 hours distributed fortnightly throughout the year during the period that teachers are engaged in more than 400 hours of Reading Recovery teaching.

Training for tutors of teachers, who guide the Reading Recovery programme in their district, is a national, year-long University and College of Education-based course which assumes that the tutor will also work as a Reading Recovery teacher for part of her day.

A national network of tutors is trained and led by a Director and several National Co-ordinators who foster professional development among all Reading Recovery professionals and run training courses for new tutors.

Some recommendations

The research studies point to some recommendations for Reading Recovery teachers, and their schools.

1   When children are to be included in a Reading Recovery programme contact parents and contract for regular attendance for this second-chance learning opportunity. The school should cooperate with the family to establish appropriate home activities to follow up on lessons.

2   Allow for sufficient time in the programme and apply discontinuing criteria conservatively especially with the Maori children.

3   Adopt a watch-dog role for ex-Reading Recovery children in the school and remind staff

- to monitor their progress sensitively
- to consider their promotion carefully
- to provide further individual help if needed and particularly if progress is slow.

Although Reading Recovery children may perform well in their classes they remain at-risk children for two or more years after completion of their programme.

Readers with problems

Once this programme is fully implemented its impact within the education system will be felt as each age group moves up through the primary school. There should be a drastic reduction in the numbers of children requiring special teaching for fundamental skills in reading and writing above the second year at school. Many more of the 'slow' children in schools should be able to perform close to average class levels in reading and writing and be able to use these achievements in the service of further learning. This programme will also contribute to the early identification, by six-and-a-half years or eighteen months from school entry, of Referred children requiring the attention of a reading specialist for at least a further year or two.

Gains for the education system

Some of the inefficiencies that have seemed unavoidable in the past should disappear. We should reduce the problems of the teacher in the upper primary or elementary school who tries to teach a non-reader but does not really know how to; the time spent by teachers with the 'low reading groups' should be reduced; the number of children on waiting lists for reading clinics should be reduced. Hopefully children needing continuing help should be able to move straight from Reading Recovery to a reading specialist and not have to wait for a place marking time in a classroom where the programme is beyond them.

Because the effects of the programme run counter to past experience it seems unwise to make undue claims for it. However, the three-year follow-up research which suggests that for those having daily instruction in Reading Recovery the long-term effects were good for each of three ethnic groups, European, Maori and Pacific Island children, is supported by two other follow-up studies in Victoria, Australia and Ohio, USA.

The cost-effectiveness of the programme depends upon how well it achieves its goal of average performance for most of the children. The programme addresses a problem of Western education systems in that it provides for all children at the lower end of the achievement distribution at six years to receive supplementary help with literacy learning. It runs with a minimum of specialist staff. Most importantly, it is a targeted education programme which, if it works, reduces the need for specialist provision in the upper primary (or elementary) school and secondary school.

It has been an exciting exploration of the question 'What is possible when we change the design and delivery of traditional education for the children that teachers find hard to teach?'

BIBLIOGRAPHY FOR READING RECOVERY

(References cited in the text are on page 109)

RESEARCH

Anderson, R. C. 'The Ohio Reading Recovery Project: Preliminary Report of the National Evaluation Panel'. Department of Education, Columbus, Ohio, 1988.

Center, Y., Wheldall, K. and Freeman, L. 'Evaluating the effectiveness of Reading Recovery: a critique'. *Educational Psychology* 12 (3 & 4): pp 263–274, 1992.

Clay, M. M. 'Reading Recovery: a follow-up study'. In Clay, M. (Ed.) *Observing Young Readers: Selected Papers*, Heinemann Inc., Portsmouth, NH, 1982.

Clay, M. M. *The Early Detection of Reading Difficulties*, 3rd ed., Heinemann, Auckland, 1985.

Clay, M. M. 'The Reading Recovery Research Reports: Part 1'. *Reading – Canada – Lecture* 4 (2): pp 92–112, 1986.

Clay, M. M. 'The Reading Recovery Research Reports: Part 2'. *Reading – Canada – Lecture* 4 (3): pp 158–170, 1986.

Clay, M. M. 'The Reading Recovery programme, 1984–88: coverage, outcomes and Education Board district figures'. *New Zealand Journal of Educational Studies* 25 (1): pp 61–70, 1990. Also in *Oideas, Earrach*, 40: pp 21–34, 1993.

Clay, M. M. 'Syntactic awareness and Reading Recovery: a response to Tunmer'. *New Zealand Journal of Educational Studies* 26 (1): pp 87–91, 1991.

Clay, M. M. and Tuck, B. *A Study of Reading Recovery Subgroups: Including Outcomes for Children Who Did Not Satisfy Discontinuing Criteria*, University of Auckland, Auckland, New Zealand, 1991.

Clay, M. M. and Watson, B. 'The Success of Maori Children in the Reading Recovery Programme'. Report to the Director of Research, Department of Education, Wellington, 1982.

Clough, M., McIntyre, J. and Cowey, W. *Canberra Word Test*, University of Canberra, Schools and Community Centre, 1990.

Cohen, S. G., McDonell, G. and Osborn, B. 'Self-perceptions of "at risk" and high achieving readers: beyond Reading Recovery achievement data'. *Cognitive and Social Perspectives for Literacy Research and Instruction*, National Reading Conference Yearbook, National Reading Conference, Chicago, 1989.

DeFord, D. E. 'An exploration of text reading and reading group placement of third-grade students'. Proceedings of the 32nd National Reading Conference, December 1988. National Reading Conference, Chicago, 1990.

Demetre, J. D. 'A Review of Evaluation Studies of the Reading Recovery Programme'. Institute of Education, University of London (CDPE), submitted for publication, 1993.

Escamilla, K. *An Application of Reading Recovery in Spanish*. Report prepared for the Office of Educational Research and Improvement (OERI) from a grant provided by the OERI Fellows Program 1991–92, 1992.

Escamilla, K. and Andrade, A. 'An application of Reading Recovery in Spanish'. *Education and Urban Society* 24 (2): pp 213–226, 1992.

Foster, K. Critique of *Reading Recovery in Context: A Response* (personal communication to M. Clay), 1989.

Geekie, P. 'Reading Recovery: It's not what you do it's the way you do it'. In Jones, N. and Baglin Jones, E. (Eds) *Learning to Behave: Curriculum and Whole School Management Approaches to Discipline*, pp 170–188, Kogan Page, London, 1992.

Glynn, T., Bethune, N., Crooks, T., Ballard, K. and Smith, J. 'Reading Recovery in Context: implementation and outcome'. *Educational Psychology* 12 (3 & 4): pp 249–261, 1992.

Glynn, T., Crooks, T., Bethune, N., Ballard, K. and Smith J. *Reading Recovery in Context*. Report to Research Division, Ministry of Education, Wellington, 1989.

Gregory, D., Earl, L. and Donoghue, B. *A Study of Reading Recovery in Scarborough: 1990–1992*, Research Centre, Scarborough Board of Education, Scarborough, Ontario, 1993.

Huck, C. S. and Pinnell, G. S. *The Reading Recovery Project in Columbus Ohio: Pilot Year, 1984–1985*. Technical Report, The Ohio State University, Columbus, Ohio, 1985.

Iversen, S. J. 'Phonological Processing Skills and the Reading Recovery Programme'. MA dissertation Library of Massey University, Palmerston North, New Zealand, 1991.

Iversen, S. and Tunmer, W. E. 'Phonological processing skills and the Reading Recovery program'. *Journal of Educational Psychology* 85 (1): pp 112–126, 1993.

Lyons, C. A. 'Reading Recovery: A preventative for mislabeling young "at-risk" learners'. *Urban Education* 24 (2): pp 125–139, 1989. (Reprinted 1989, *Spectrum: Journal of School Research and Information* 7: pp 3–9.) (Reprinted 1990, *Educational Research Digest.)*

Lyons, C. A. 'A comparative study of the teaching effectiveness of teachers participating in a year-long or two-week inservice program'. In Zutell, J and McCormick, S. (Eds) *Learner Factors/Teacher Factors: Issues in Literacy Research and Instruction,* Fortieth edition of the National Reading Conference Yearbook, National Reading Conference, Chicago, 1991.

Lyons, C. A. and Beaver, J. 'Reducing retention and learning disability placement through Reading Recovery: an educationally sound, cost-effective choice'. In Allington, R. L. and Walmsley, S. A. (Eds) *No Quick Fix: Redesigning Literacy Programs in America's Elementary Schools,* Teachers College Press, New York, NY, 1993.

McCormack, M. J. *How Well do Maori Children Recover after Reading Recovery?* Research Report No. 90–2, Education Department, University of Canterbury, 1990.

Moore, M. and Wade, B. 'Reading Recovery: parents' views.'*English in Education* 27(2): pp 11–17, 1993.

New Zealand Ministry of Education. 'Annual Summaries of Reading Recovery Data', *Research and Statistics Division Bulletins*, May 1991, May 1992, November 1992 and May 1993'. Research and Statistics Division, Wellington.

Nicholson, T. 'A comment on Reading Recovery'. *New Zealand Journal of Educational Studies* 24 (1): pp 95–97, 1989.

Ohio State University. *Ohio's Reading Recovery Program.* The Ohio State University, Columbus, Ohio, 1991.

Ohio State University. *Reading Recovery Executive Summary.* The Ohio State University, Columbus, Ohio, 1992.

Pinnell, G. S. 'Reading Recovery: helping at-risk children learn to read'. *The Elementary School Journal* 90 (2): pp 161–183, University of Chicago, Chicago, 1990.

Pinnell, G. S., DeFord, D. E. and Lyons, C. A. *Reading Recovery: Early Intervention for At-Risk First Graders,* Educational Research Service Monograph, Educational Research Service, Arlington, Virginia, 1988.

Pinnell, G. S., Lyons, C. A., DeFord, D. E., Bryk, A. S. and Seltzer, M. *Studying the Effectiveness of Early Intervention Approaches for First Grade Children Having Difficulty in Reading.* Educational Report No. 16, The Ohio State University, Columbus, Ohio, 1991.

Pluck, M. L. 'Reading Recovery in a British infant school'. *Educational Psychology* 9 (4): 1989.

Rentel, V. M. and Pinnell, G. S. *A Study of Practical Reasoning in Reading Recovery Instruction.* Paper presented at the National Reading Conference, December, 1987.

Rowe, K. 'Literacy Programs Study: Reading Recovery'. Ministry of Education, Melbourne, Victoria, 1988.

Searfoss, L. W. and Enz, B. J. 'Collaborative Literacy Intervention Project First Year Report Summary'. Arizona State University, Tempe, Arizona, 1991.

Smith, J. 'Reading Recovery in central Victoria: what we have learnt'. *Australian Journal of Reading* 9 (4): pp 201–208, 1986.

Stringfield, S. 'Special Studies Project: First, Second and Third Year Reports'. Center for Social Organization of Schools, John Hopkins University, Baltimore, MD, submitted to the US Office of Education for publication, 1993.

Surrey County Council. *Reading Recovery: Initial Evaluation.* Surrey County Council, Kingston-on-Thames, 1991.

Technical Report Vol. 1. Huck, C. and Pinnell, G. *The Reading Recovery Project in Columbus, Ohio: Pilot Year, 1984–85,* The Ohio State University, Columbus, Ohio, 1985.

Technical Report Vol. 2. Pinnell, G., Short, K., Lyons, C. A. and Young, P. *The Ohio Reading Recovery Project: Follow-up Study in Columbus, Ohio, 1985–86,* The Ohio State University, Columbus, Ohio, 1986.

Technical Report Vol. 3. Pinnell, G., Short, K., Lyons, C. A. and Young, P. *The Reading Recovery Project in Columbus, Ohio: 1985–86,* The Ohio State University, Columbus, Ohio, 1986.

Technical Report Vol. 4. Lyons, C. A., Pinnell, G., Short, K. and Young, P. *The (State of) Ohio Reading Recovery Project: Pilot Year, 1985–86,* The Ohio State University, Columbus, Ohio, 1986.

Technical Report Vol. 6. Pinnell, G. S., Lyons, C. A., Young, P. and Deford, D. *The Reading Recovery Project in Columbus, Ohio, Year 2, 1986–87,* The Ohio State University, Columbus, Ohio, 1987.

Technical Report Vol. 7. Deford, D., Pinnell, G. S., Lyons, C. A. and Young, P. *Report of the Follow-up Studies: Columbus, 1985–86 and 1986–87,* The Ohio State University, Columbus, Ohio, 1987.

Technical Report Vol. 8. Lyons, C., Pinnell, G. S., McCarrier, A., Young, P. and Deford, D. *The Ohio Reading Recovery Project, 1986–87*, The Ohio State University, Columbus, Ohio, 1987.

Tunmer, W. E. 'The role of language prediction skills in beginning reading'. *New Zealand Journal of Educational Studies* 25 (2): pp 95–113, 1990.

Tunmer, W. E. 'Phonological processing and Reading Recovery: a reply to Clay'. *New Zealand Journal of Educational Studies* 27 (2): pp 203–217, 1992.

Wheeler, H. *Reading Recovery: Central Victorian Field Trials 1984*, Bendigo College of Advanced Education, Bendigo, 1986.

Wright, A. 'Evaluation of the first British Reading Recovery programme'. *British Educational Research Journal* 18 (4): pp 351–368, 1992.

Wright, A. 'The Views of Parents and Teachers Involved in the First British Reading Recovery Programme'. In press, 1993.

BOOKS
(About, or with important references to the programme)

Clay, M. M. *Observing Young Readers: Selected Papers*, Heinemann Inc., Portsmouth, NH, 1982.

Clay, M. M. *Becoming Literate: the Construction of Inner Control*, Heinemann, Auckland, 1991.

Cline, T. (Ed.) *The Assessment of Special Educational Needs: International Perspectives*, Routledge, London, 1992. Chapter by Clay, M. M. 'A second chance to learn literacy: by different routes to common outcomes (The Reading Recovery Programme)', pp 69–89.

DeFord, D. E., Lyons, C. A. and Pinnell, G. S. *Bridges to Literacy: Learning from Reading Recovery*, Heinemann Inc., Portsmouth, NH, 1991.

Lyons, C. A., Pinnell, G. S. and DeFord, D. E. *Partners in Learning: Teachers and Children in Reading Recovery*. In press, 1993.

Ofsted Report. *Reading Recovery in New Zealand. A Report from the Office of Her Majesty's Chief Inspector of Schools*, HMSO, London, 1993.

Watson, A. and Badenhop, A. (Eds) *Prevention of Reading Failure*, Ashton Scholastic, Gosford, 1992. Chapter by Clay, M. M. 'Preventing reading failure: the wider implications of an educational innovation', pp 22–47.

ARTICLES AND CHAPTERS

Adams, M. J. *Beginning to Read: Thinking and Learning about Print*, MIT Press, Cambridge, Mass., 1990.

Allington, R. L. and Johnston, P. 'Coordination, collaboration, and consistency: the redesign of compensatory and special education interventions'. In Slavin, R. E. et al. *Effective Programs for Students At Risk*, Allyn and Bacon, Needham Heights, Mass., 1989.

Allington, R. L. and McGill-Franzen, A. 'Children with reading problems: how we wrongfully classify them and fail to teach many to read.' *ERS Research Digest*, ERS, Arlington, Virginia, 1990.

Asmussen, L. and Gaffney, J. S. 'Reading in families: a research update'. *Reading Horizons* 31 (5): pp 449–452, Western Michigan University, Michigan, 1991.

Barnett, W.S. and Escobar, C. M. 'The economics of early educational intervention: a review'. *Review of Educational Research* 57: pp 384–414, 1987.

Boehmein, M. 'Reading intervention for high-risk first graders'. *Educational Leadership* 44: pp 32–37, 1987.

Cazden, C. B. 'Revealing and telling: the socialisation of attention in learning to read and write'. *Educational Psychology* 12 (3 & 4): pp 305–313, 1992.

Clark, M. M. 'Sensitive observation and the development of literacy'. *Educational Psychology* 12 (3 & 4): pp 215–223, 1992.

Clay, M. M. 'Learning to be learning disabled'. *New Zealand Journal of Educational Studies* 22 (2): pp 155–173, 1987.

Clay, M. M. 'Implementing Reading Recovery: systemic adaptions to an educational innovation'. *New Zealand Journal of Educational Studies* 22 (1): pp 35–58, 1987.

Clay, M. M. *Studying Developmental Change with a Successful Intervention*. Paper presented at the Fifth Australian Developmental Conference in affiliation with the International Congress of Psychology, Sydney, Australia, 1988.

Clay, M. M. *Reading Recovery in the United States: Its Successes and Challenges*. Paper presented at the AERA Annual Meeting, Division C; SIG/Basic Research in Reading. Boston, Mass., 1990. (ERIC Resources.)

Clay, M. M. 'Learning to be learning disabled'. *Spectrum: Journal of School Research and Information* 8 (3): Summer 1990. Also, *ERS Research Digest*, 1990.

Clay, M. M. 'Reading Recovery surprises'. In DeFord, D. E., Lyons, C. A. and Pinnell, G. S. (Eds) *Bridges to Literacy: Learning from Reading Recovery*, Heinemann Inc., Portsmouth, NH, 1991.

Clay, M. M. 'Why is an inservice programme for Reading Recovery teachers necessary?' *Reading Horizons* 31(5): pp 355–372, Western Michigan University, Michigan, 1991.

Clay, M. M. 'Introducing a new storybook to young readers'. *The Reading Teacher* 45 (4): pp 264–273, 1991.

Clay, M. M. and Cazden, C. B. 'A Vygotskian interpretation of Reading Recovery'. In Moll, L.C. (Ed.) *Vygotsky and Education: Instructional Implications and Applications of Socio-historical Psychology*, Cambridge University Press, Cambridge, 1990.

Clay, M. M. and Watson, B. 'An in-service programme for Reading Recovery teachers'. *Education* 4: pp 22–27. Reprinted in *Observing Young Readers*, Heinemann Inc., Portsmouth, NH, 1982.

DeFord, D. E. 'Using reading and writing to support the reader'. In DeFord, D. E., Lyons, C. A. and Pinnell, G. S. (Eds) *Bridges to Literacy: Learning from Reading Recovery,* Heinemann Inc., Portsmouth, NH, 1991.

DeFord, D. E. 'Fluency in initial reading instruction: a Reading Recovery lesson'. *Theory into Practice* 15 (3): Summer 1991, Ohio State University College of Education, 1991.

Dunkeld, C. *Gaining Experience with Reading Recovery: A Pilot Project Between Portland Public Schools and Portland State University*, Portland State University, Portland, OR., 1990.

Dunkeld, C. 'Maintaining the integrity of a promising program: the case of Reading Recovery'. In DeFord, D. E., Lyons, C. A. and Pinnell, G. S. (Eds) *Bridges to Literacy: Learning from Reading Recovery*, pp 37–54, Heinemann Inc., Portsmouth, NH, 1991.

Dunkeld, C. and Dunbar, Z. 'The early detection of reading difficulty: the use of Marie Clay's diagnostic survey and Reading Recovery procedures with first grade children'. *Resources in Education*, Ed 301 846, 1983.

Dyer, P. C. 'Reading Recovery: a cost-effectiveness and educational-outcomes analysis'. *ERS Spectrum*, 10 (1): pp 10–19, 1992.

Elkins, J. 'The nurture of reading: implications for special education'. *Educational Psychology* 12 (3 & 4): pp 291–303, 1992.

Gaffney, J. S. 'Reading Recovery: getting started in a school system'. *Reading Horizons* 31 (5): pp 373–383, Western Michigan University, Michigan, 1991.

Gaffney, J. S. and Anderson, R. C. *Two-Tiered Scaffolding: Congruent Processes of Teaching and Learning.* Technical Report No. 523, Center for the Study of Reading, University of Illinois at Urbana-Champaign, Illinois, 1991.

Glynn, T. and McNaughton, S. 'Early literacy learning: a tribute to Marie Clay'. *Educational Psychology* 12 (3 & 4): pp 171–176, 1992.

Hamill, J., Kelly, C. and Jacobson. 'As we see it; classroom teachers view Reading Recovery'. *Reading Horizons* 31 (5): pp 439–448, Western Michigan University, Michigan, 1991.

Holland, K. E. 'Bringing home and school literacy together through the Reading Recovery program'. In Deford, D. E., Lyons, C. A. and Pinnell, G. S. (Eds) *Bridges to Literacy: Learning from Reading Recovery*, pp 149–170, Heinemann Inc., Portsmouth, NH, 1991.

Huck, C. S. and Pinnell, G. S. 'Literacy in the classroom'. In DeFord, D. E., Lyons, C. A. and Pinnell, G. S. (Eds) *Bridges to Literacy: Learning from Reading Recovery*, pp 217–231, Heinemann Inc., Portsmouth, NH, 1991.

Jones, N. K. 'Helping to learn: components and principles of Reading Recovery training'. *Reading Horizons* 31 (5): pp. 421–438, Western Michigan University, Michigan, 1991.

Lyons, C. A. 'Reading Recovery: an effective early intervention program that can prevent mislabeling children as learning disabled'. *ERS Research Digest*, ERS, Arlington, Virginia, 1990.

Lyons, C. A. 'Reading Recovery: a viable prevention of learning disability'. *Reading Horizons* 31 (5): pp 384–408, Western Michigan University, Michigan, 1991.

Lyons, C. A. 'Helping a learning-disabled child enter the literate world'. In DeFord, D. E., Lyons, C. A. and Pinnell, G. S. (Eds) *Bridges to Literacy: Learning from Reading Recovery*, pp 205–216, Heinemann Inc., Portsmouth, NH, 1991.

Madden, N. A. and Slavin, R. E. 'Effective pullout programs for students at risk'. In Slavin, R. E. et al. *Effective Programs for Students at Risk*, Allyn and Bacon, Needham Heights, Mass, 1989.

Ohio State University, College of Education. 'Reading Recovery 1984–1989.' *National Diffusion Network* 4: pp 1–12, 1989.

Opitz, M. F. 'Hypothesizing about Reading Recovery'. *Reading Horizons* 31 (5): pp 409–420, Western Michigan University, Michigan, 1991.

Peterson, B. 'Selecting books for beginning readers'. In DeFord, D. E., Lyons, C. A. and Pinnell, G. S. (Eds). *Bridges to Literacy: Learning from Reading Recovery*, pp 119–138, Heinemann Inc., Portsmouth, NH, 1991.

Pinnell, G. S. 'Holistic ways to help children at risk of failure'. *Teachers Networking: The Whole Language Newsletter* 9 (1): pp 9–12, 1988.

Pinnell, G. S. 'Reading Recovery: helping at-risk children learn to read'. *Elementary School Journal* 90 (2): pp 161–183, 1989.

Pinnell, G. S. 'Success for low achievers through Reading Recovery'. *Educational Leadership* 48 (1): pp 17–21, 1990.

Pinnell, G. S. 'Teachers and children learning'. In DeFord, D. E., Lyons, C. A. and Pinnell, G. S. (Eds) *Bridges to Literacy: Learning from Reading Recovery*, pp 171–188, Heinemann Inc., Portsmouth, NH, 1991.

Pinnell, G. S., Fried, M. D., and Estice, R. M. 'Reading Recovery: learning how to make a difference'. *The Reading Teacher*, January, 1990, pp 282–295. Also in Deford, D. E., Lyons, C. A. and Pinnell, G. S. (Eds) *Bridges to Literacy: Learning from Reading Recovery*, pp 97–118, Heinemann Inc., Portsmouth, NH, 1990.

Robinson, V. 'Some limitations of systemic adaptation: the implementation of Reading Recovery'. *New Zealand Journal of Educational Studies* 24 (1): 35–45, 1989.

Short, K. G. 'Literacy environments that support strategic readers'. In DeFord, D. E., Lyons, C. A. and Pinnell, G. S. (Eds) *Bridges to Literacy: Learning from Reading Recovery*, pp 97–118. Heinemann Inc., Portsmouth, NH, 1991.

Slavin, R. E. 'Making chapter 1 make a difference'. *Phi Delta Kappan* 69 (2): pp 110–119, 1987.

Wasik, B. A. and Slavin, R. E. 'Preventing early reading failure with one-to-one tutoring: a review of five programs'. *Reading Research Quarterly* 28(2): pp 178–190, 1993.

Woolsey, D. P. 'Changing contexts for literacy learning: the impact of Reading Recovery on one first-grade teacher'. In DeFord, D. E., Lyons, C. A. and Pinnell, G. S. (Eds) *Bridges to Literacy: Learning from Reading Recovery*, pp 187–204, Heinemann Inc., Portsmouth, NH, 1991.

Yukish, J. 'Reading Recovery: early help for at-risk readers'. *Updating School Board Policies* 19 (4): pp 2–4, 1988.

APPENDICES

WEEKLY RECORD OF WRITING VOCABULARY

Name: _____

Date of Birth: _____

Initial Testing: Date:	Week: Date:	Week: Date:	Week: Date:	Week: Date:	Week: Date:
Week: Date:	Week: Date:	Week: Date:	Week: Date:	Week: Date:	

LESSON RECORD

NAME: _____ DATE: _____

READING				
NEW TEXT	RE-READING	STRATEGIES 1 USED 2 PROMPTED	TAKING WORDS APART IN READING	1 LETTER IDENTIFICATION 2 MAKING AND BREAKING

WRITING			CUT-UP STORY		
TASK	CONSTRUCTING WORDS AND FLUENCY PRACTICE	SPATIAL CONCEPTS	SEQUENCING	COMMENT

RECOMMENDATIONS FOR DISCONTINUING CHILDREN

Name: _____

Date: _____

School: _____

1   SETTING (Same class, new class, book level, teacher's reaction, size of group etc.)

2   SURVIVAL (Detail what behaviours will ensure coping in group instruction)

3   RUNNING RECORD ANALYSIS (Detail cues used and cues neglected)

4   COMMENT ON IMPROVEMENTS SINCE PREVIOUS SUMMARY AND PREDICTIONS

RECOMMENDATIONS: (for class teacher, or further teaching or further assessment)

Signed: _____

OBSERVATION SUMMARY FOR MULTIPLE TESTINGS

Name: _____

Date of Birth: _____

School: _____

SUMMARY OF RUNNING RECORD

	Text Titles	Running words Error	Error rate	Accuracy	Self-correction rate

Initial Test   Date: _____

1. Easy _____ _____ 1: _____ _____ % 1: _____

2. Instructional _____ _____ 1: _____ _____ % 1: _____

3. Hard _____ _____ 1: _____ _____ % 1: _____

Retest   Date: _____

1. Easy _____ _____ 1: _____ _____ % 1: _____

2. Instructional _____ _____ 1: _____ _____ % 1: _____

3. Hard _____ _____ 1: _____ _____ % 1: _____

Further Test   Date: _____

1. Easy _____ _____ 1: _____ _____ % 1: _____

2. Instructional _____ _____ 1: _____ _____ % 1: _____

3. Hard _____ _____ 1: _____ _____ % 1: _____

TESTS	L.I. 54	Stanine	C.A.P. 24	Stanine	Word Test 15	Stanine	Reading Test Score	Writing	Stanine	Hearing Sounds in Words 37	Stanine
Initial test Date:											
Retest Date:											
Further Test (1)											
Further Test (2)											

RECOMMENDATIONS: (for class teacher, or for review, or further teaching, or further assessment)

REFERENCES

Bradley, L. *Assessing Reading Difficulties: A Diagnostic and Remedial Approach*. Macmillan, London, 1980.

Clay, Marie M. 'Emergent Reading Behaviour'. Unpubl. doctoral dissertation, University of Auckland Library, Auckland, 1966.

Clay, Marie M. *Reading: The Patterning of Complex Behaviour*, 2nd ed., Heinemann, Auckland, 1979.

Clay, Marie M. *Observing Young Readers: Selected Papers*, Heinemann Inc., Portsmouth, NH, 1982.

Clay, Marie M. *The Early Detection of Reading Difficulties*, 3rd ed., Heinemann, Auckland, 1985.

Clay, Marie M. 'Reading Recovery: systemic adaptations to an educational innovation'. *New Zealand Journal of Educational Studies* 22(1): pp 35–58, 1987.

Clay, Marie M. 'The Reading Recovery Programme, 1984–88: coverage, outcomes and Education Board figures'. *New Zealand Journal of Educational Studies* 25(1): pp 61–70, 1990.

Clay, Marie M. *Becoming Literate: The Construction of Inner Control*, Heinemann, Auckland, 1991a.

Clay, Marie M. 'Introducing a storybook to young readers'. *The Reading Teacher* 45(4): pp 264–273, 1991b.

Clay, Marie M. *An Observation Survey of Early Literacy Achievement*, Heinemann, Auckland, 1993.

Clay, M.M. and Tuck, B. 'A Study of Reading Recovery Subgroups: Including Outcomes for Children Who Did Not Satisfy Discontinuing Criteria', University of Auckland, Auckland, 1991.

Clay, Marie M. and Watson, B. 'The Success of Maori Children in the Reading Recovery Programme'. Report to the Director of Research, Department of Education, Wellington, 1982.

Ehri, L. C. and Sweet, J. 'Fingerpoint-reading of memorized text: what enables beginners to process the print?' *Reading Research Quarterly* 26(4): pp 442–462, 1991.

Fernald, G. M. *Remedial Techniques in Basic School Subjects*, McGraw-Hill, New York, 1943.

Glynn, I., Crookes, I., Bethune, N., Ballard, K. and

Smith, J. 'Reading Recovery in Context'. Report to Research Division, Ministry of Education, Wellington, 1989.

Iversen, S. J. 'Phonological processing skills and the Reading Recovery programme'. MA dissertation, Massey University Library, Palmerston North, NZ, 1991.

Neale, Marie D. *The Neale Analysis of Reading Ability*, Macmillan, London, 1958. (Restandardised by Macmillan, 1988; and NFER, 1989.)

New Zealand Council for Educational Research. *Burt Word Reading Test*, NZCER, Wellington, 1981.

New Zealand Department of Education. *LARIC Inservice Programme*, Learning Media, Wellington, 1984.

New Zealand Department of Education. *Tomorrow's Schools*, Government Printer, Wellington, 1988.

New Zealand Ministry of Education. 'Ready to Read' series, 1st ed., Learning Media, Wellington, 1963.

Nicholson, T. 'Research note: a comment on Reading Recovery'. *New Zealand Journal of Educational Studies* 24: pp 95–97, 1989.

Peters, M. L. *Success in Spelling*, Cambridge Institute of Education, Cambridge, 1970.

Pinnell, G. S., DeFord, D. E. and Lyons, C. A. *Reading Recovery: Early Intervention for At-risk First Graders*, Educational Research Service, Arlington, Va, 1988.

Robinson, Susan M. 'Predicting Early Reading Progress'. Unpubl. MA thesis, University of Auckland Library, Auckland, 1973.

Strickland, D. and Morrow, L. M. (Eds). *Emerging Literacy: Young Children Learn to Read and Write*, International Reading Association, Newark, DE, 1989.

Wade, T. 'Promotion Patterns in the Junior School'. Unpubl. Dip. Ed. thesis, University of Auckland Library, Auckland, 1978.

Wheeler, H. *Reading Recovery: Central Victorian Field Trials, 1984*, Bendigo College of Advanced Education, Bendigo, 1986.

INDEX